Inherent Human Dignity

THE BEGINNING AND THE BEYOND OF POLITICS

Series editors: James R. Stoner and David Walsh

The series is in continuity with the grand tradition of political philosophy that was revitalized by the scholars who, after the Second World War, taught us to return to the past as a means of understanding the present. We are convinced that legal and constitutional issues cannot be addressed without acknowledging the metaphysical dimensions that underpin them. Questions of order arise within a cosmos that invites us to wonder about its beginning and its end, while drawing out the consequences for the way we order our lives together. God and man, world and society are the abiding partners within the community of being in which we find ourselves. Without limiting authors to any particular framework we welcome all who wish to investigate politics in the widest possible horizon.

GLENN HUGHES

Inherent Human Dignity

A PHILOSOPHICAL MEDITATION

University of Notre Dame Press
Notre Dame, Indiana

University of Notre Dame Press
Notre Dame, Indiana 46556
undpress.nd.edu

All Rights Reserved

Copyright © 2025 by the University of Notre Dame

Published in the United States of America

Library of Congress Control Number: 2025934546

ISBN: 978-0-268-20996-4 (Hardback)
ISBN: 978-0-268-20995-7 (Paperback)
ISBN: 978-0-268-20993-3 (WebPDF)
ISBN: 978-0-268-20994-0 (Epub3)

GPSR Compliance Inquiries:
Lightning Source France, 1 Av. Johannes Gutenberg, 78310 Maurepas, France
compliance@lightningsource.fr | Phone: +33 1 30 49 23 42

for
Henrik Syse

I write to justify myself in the eyes of the child I was.
—Georges Bernanos

CONTENTS

Foreword, by James Greenaway   xi
Preface   xvii

Part 1. Preliminaries

ONE	Honesty	3
TWO	Meaning and Value	7
THREE	The Cosmos	11
FOUR	Belonging	15
FIVE	The Desire to Know	20
SIX	Myth	25
SEVEN	The World of Space and Time	30
EIGHT	Science	35
NINE	Misunderstanding Human Nature	41
TEN	Constants of Human Nature	47

Part 2. The Idea of Inherent Human Dignity

ELEVEN	Inherent Human Dignity	55
TWELVE	Inherent Dignity in the Universal Declaration of Human Rights (I)	61
THIRTEEN	Inherent Dignity in the Universal Declaration of Human Rights (II)	66
FOURTEEN	Persons, Rights, and Dignified Living	71
FIFTEEN	Digression: The Universal Search for Dignified Living	76
SIXTEEN	The Challenge of Respecting Inherent Dignity	81
SEVENTEEN	Transcendent Mystery and Shakenness	86
EIGHTEEN	Eclipsing Transcendent Mystery	91
NINETEEN	Inherent Dignity as Both Concept and Mythic Symbol	96
TWENTY	The Refusal to Understand Inherent Dignity	102
TWENTY-ONE	Inherent Dignity and Ideology	106
EPILOGUE	Love and Inherent Dignity	111

Notes   115
Bibliography   121
Index   125

FOREWORD

James Greenaway

Glenn "Chip" Hughes will be no stranger to many who read this book. For those of us who have known and loved him, the book will be readily recognized as something of a philosophical biography. For those who have not met him, *Inherent Human Dignity* will serve as both an introduction to his thought and a mature statement on the direction and concern of all of his philosophical writings.

This relatively short text, however, does not function merely as a record of a man's philosophical life and development. It brings something new to the field of human dignity studies. Hughes, in thinking through his own set of foundational insights, has presented a coherent argument for why the idea of equal inherent dignity is so central to our political and cultural lives together. Many of us find that we already have a commitment to the value of the person and the common good—a conviction about the inviolable worth of any person and community—that makes us wary of collectivisms, reductionisms, and other modes of thinking and behavior that tilt in the direction of human degradation. Hughes brings this abiding, often implicit, conviction to the forefront and asks us to accompany him as he sets about exploring the philosophical basis for such a belief. Prescinding from religious and metaphysical claims, no matter how complementary, he articulates such a basis as grounded in the experience of being human. Importantly, through this experience, each of us has access to the constancy and universality of being human that such religious and metaphysical claims can then elaborate. Each of us, if we choose to do the hard work of thinking about our humanity, is able to affirm the reality of equal inherent human dignity. Thus, the themes of honesty and authenticity run through Hughes's analysis, challenging the reader to grasp and to appropriate not simply the conceptual narrative of the book, but more precisely the "data" of their own personal experience of being human that underpins the narrative.

If the reader considers the question, "Why does the worth of a human being lie beyond any cost-benefit calculation?" to be an important one, then he or she will surely find Hughes's exploration of equal inherent human dignity in this book to be relevant and important. Indeed, it is likely to become the standard point of reference for those seeking a deeper, more existentially rich engagement with the idea of inherent dignity.

Hughes intended that the book be accessible to an intelligent, nonacademic audience. It is written as a series of brief, targeted reflections, each picking up from the one before. Hughes has divided it into two parts. Part 1, "Preliminaries," lays out an understanding of the foundational concepts in play in the idea of inherent human dignity. These foundational concepts are not the sophisticated jargon of academic scholarship, but the stuff of human life, grounded in experience. The reader is invited to search one's own self attentively for the data that such concepts communicate. Part 2, "The Idea of Inherent Human Dignity," proceeds to a contextualization of human dignity within the shifting political, historical, and philosophical horizons of humanity. Hughes, masterful teacher and writer, guides the reader to explore their own personal interiority as well as the political and cultural manifestations of being human in their own time and place, and perennially in the cosmos.

A hallmark of Hughes's style over the years is the employ of attractive images and brilliant—and often witty—insights. The present work is no exception. It is worth pointing out that Hughes has always taken his readers seriously. In so doing, he presents the material here with the presumption that the reader is an interlocutor worth conversing with. The warm, conversational manner in which the book proceeds is quite intentional, as though Hughes were wanting to sit down with his fellow human beings to speak with them, perhaps to edify and uplift them, convinced that the mutuality of philosophical friendship is both an end worth striving for and the means of overcoming all that would make us narrow, petty, and resentful. Hughes wants his readers to think along with him. When he asks, for example, whether the idea of equal inherent dignity is more than simply an idea, not simply a notion in the mind, but rather a fact, something real that we must not ignore, he is also asking of himself a question that is "existentially charged—because if the answer to the . . . question is yes, then the result will be that the inquirer affirms as true something that has major consequences for how he or she should live, regard others, and understand his situation in the cosmos."

Many of the predominant themes across Hughes's career appear here in concise form. I will mention two. The first is what he himself referred to as "participationalist metaphysics," by which he means a way of thinking about reality as that to which we fundamentally belong by our own existence. By simply existing, we are already participating in the encompassing Whole of reality that we can call the cosmos. Reality is not a thing "out there" while I remain "in here," as though the human project of thinking and seeking meaning is one of "confronting" reality. Rather, by participation, the human "place" in the cosmos is already "in between" the two primordial dimensions of reality that we exist within and exist as part of: the spatiotemporal dimension of "immanence" and the mysterious dimension of "transcendence." Existence is participation in the cosmos, not confrontation. This has inspired Hughes to read, teach, and write about the constants of human nature across all peoples of all times with humility and reverence, and he has drawn from some of the most significant philosophers of the past and present to bring out what is enduring in their works. In the scholarly communities that have assembled around the works of Eric Voegelin and Bernard Lonergan, Hughes found a home among friends. He presents the fruit of that philosophical friendship here in a way that is accessible and open to all.

Another theme that announces its presence is the possibility of ignorance and error that sometimes becomes mendacious and murderous. With eyes wide open to the bloodlust of the twentieth century, and the recurrent dogmatic and ideological biases operative in our own days, Hughes is acutely aware of human failures to be attentive, intelligent, reasonable, responsible, and loving, and of the role of philosophy (and art) in recovering sources of order in the cosmos. There is nothing in the cosmos that is higher in value than a human being because there is nothing in the cosmos that so embodies that very cosmos other than the human being. The human being is a microcosmos. To denigrate the concrete, individual person, or to use the means of institutional power to erect a goal higher in dignity than human dignity, is to disavow the cosmos and to fall into dangerous disorder. Rightly appalled at the excesses of dogmatism and ideology, and at their attendant denials of equal inherent dignity, Hughes's work can be regarded as an effort of recovery and restoration. Employing, for example, the evocative image of a tuning fork, Hughes depicts the person who participates in the encompassing cosmic Whole by his or her very existence as vibrating "with recurrent remembrance of the transcendent source of personal identity." We are more than we think we are because the infinite surplus of transcendent mystery is as much constitutive of every person as are the spatiotemporal conditions of our lives. The willed forgetfulness of being, of the cosmos, so central to ideology and existential foolishness, is contrasted here with the remembrance that is symbolized by grasping the equal inherent dignity of the person, no matter how deranged or damaged, guilty or impenitent that person may be.

"And if skepticism about current fads and modern ideologies keeps one searching; and if disgust with the existential ineptitude of those who manifest a closed-minded obeisance to religious authority doesn't prompt one on principle to abandon the search for a genuine cosmic ground, then honest efforts to remember the Mystery to which one ultimately belongs will recur." More than anything else, Hughes's own loving relationship with transcendence is the engine that has driven his thinking and writing. This is fully, and authentically, on display in this book.

Finally, it may be of interest to the reader that, within a single week in early April 2024, Hughes received two pieces of news: the first was that the University of Notre Dame Press had accepted his manuscript for publication in The Beginning and Beyond of Politics series, and the second was a diagnosis of stage 4, incurable and inoperable cancer. It happens then that this book represents the final contribution of a man who has spent his life in philosophical service to humanity. In the measured, delicate tone of one who had only just begun to absorb devastating news, he wrote in an email, "I will see if I can live up to my calling as a philosopher—one who is engaged in the practice of dying!" This is the personal context out of which *Inherent Human Dignity* comes from the author to the reader. There is nothing in this work that Hughes has not tested by his living and dying. In practicing the Platonic art of dying, Hughes has given witness to that very dignity to which he had dedicated his life exploring, unfolding, and communicating; the dignity that remained intact and integral though death drew near.

One might well consider that Hughes's career would have remained incomplete without this book, since it is here that he stands over his richly diverse literary and philosophical output and concludes that it has indeed been a unity, anchored in the idea of inherent human dignity. The epigraph, then, is well chosen. Hughes leaves us, true to the young man he was, the one who first set out to become the philosopher, and who in the end has offered so much.

Goodbye, Chip, poet and philosopher, our friend. Until we meet again.

Ave atque vale.

PREFACE

This is a philosophical book written for those who are not professional philosophers but who have philosophical questions about the concept of inherent human dignity. It was composed for readers intrigued by such questions as, Why is it reasonable to claim that humans are born with a special value—a dignity—peculiar to them? What is meant by stating that all persons are "equal in dignity"?

Awareness of the vast history of ideas opened up by such questions may so overwhelm an inquirer that exhaustion sets in before the journey properly begins. The aim of this book is to circumvent this by exploring the idea of innate, or inherent, human dignity—and the view of human nature on which it depends—in a curated sequence of brief and manageable reflections. It offers itself as both a meditation and a guide to clarify why, for many people in modern culture, the idea of human dignity has established itself both as a bedrock political fact and as a fulcrum of political critique.

My decision to write a philosophical guide to the topic—rather than a philosophical treatise—arose from a long-held desire to understand and explain as straightforwardly and accessibly as I could the notion of human dignity that is so ubiquitous in political thought and journalism. More than twenty years ago, as I was completing *Transcendence and History*, I saw that a principal motivation in writing it (though the topic is scarcely discussed in that book) was to defend the idea of universal human dignity. Upon its completion, I therefore turned to these questions: Just what is inherent human dignity? And how can affirmation of it as a fact be philosophically justified?

As these questions came into focus, I realized that I had always had a faith in the reality of this dignity, faith in an inherent human value, an innate incalculable worth, granted to each person, and always to be respected. But I saw also that I had never attempted to think through the intelligible basis of that faith. Subsequent research into scholarly treatments of the topic led me to write a handful of essays on it, which appeared in various books and journals. In the course of this work, I found that the idea had received less analysis on the part of professional philosophers than I had anticipated, especially given the ubiquity of references to human dignity in contemporary political culture and journalism. Most of the attention paid to it had come from theologians, analysts of jurisprudence, and political theorists. All of these latter thinkers used philosophical tools, of course, and often displayed exceptional philosophical acumen. But still, I was struck by the paucity of strictly philosophical analyses. I suspected that this had something to do with present-day criticism (along a number of cultural fronts) of notions of human specialness. The idea of inherent human dignity posits a distinctive value that belongs only to human beings, human persons.

It is clear why this fact has not kept Western theologians from writing on the topic: the special place of humans within creation is woven into the fabric of Jewish and Christian visions of reality. And because the idea of equal and inherent human dignity has played a significant role in the liberal tradition of Western political theory—and is increasingly written into the codes of national and international law—it continues to draw the attention of both political theorists and analysts of jurisprudence. Usually, though, these latter have focused on explaining the history of how the idea has been understood and the history of its influence, rather than on exploring its metaphysical implications. In a similar manner, contemporary philosophers treating the idea have gravitated toward explaining already-existing theories within the history of ideas (for example, analyzing Kant's accounts of dignity), rather than on both expositing and explicitly taking a stand on the idea's truth and value, and on its inevitable presuppositions and implications. To the degree that my own essays on dignity reflected this general academic tendency toward exegesis within the history of ideas, they, too, left me somewhat dissatisfied.

Out of that dissatisfaction, a distinct desire began to emerge. I found that, as useful as it had been for me to situate my questions, insights, and judgments in relation to the arguments of a host of other thinkers, modern and premodern, I wanted to bear a more direct witness to the existential progress that the production of my own essays had demanded. I decided to revisit and extend my investigations into the idea of inherent dignity in a manner that stripped away the formalities of professional style in favor of a more direct philosophical report. Also, I decided to provide a prelude to those investigations, consisting of an account of the philosophical foundations and existential commitments on which my study of the idea had been based.

Thus, this book was launched: a sequence of reflections, each of four to six pages, that starts at the beginning by setting forth what I take to be my situation as an existing human being in my given cultural-historical context, and subsequently proceeds to an examination of the idea of inherent human dignity. The initial reflections, presented in part 1, "Preliminaries," express my understanding of a key range of concepts that must be employed, it seems to me, in the analysis of that idea—concepts such as "cosmos," "participation," "transcendence," "myth," and "human nature." They set out what might be called my philosophical memory: the outlook made up of a web of philosophical judgments on which is based, in part 2, my investigation of the idea of inherent dignity. Initially, I expected that four or five such preliminary reflections would be sufficient, but, as happens so often, one insight led to another, and four or five chapters became ten.

Part 2, "The Idea of Inherent Human Dignity," examines that idea in the context of a series of metaphysical, historical, and political questions. In places, these include heavily revised material from my essays published in books and journals, and first-version chapters from both parts of this book appeared on the website VoegelinView.com.

What this short book offers to the reader is neither a treatise on the idea of inherent human dignity nor a summary of philosophical (or theological or jurisprudential or political) thinking on the topic, but a meditation in which each chapter is both a discrete study of the topic indicated by its title and part of a sequence in which each chapter's insights and formulations inform those of the chapters that follow.

At the same time, it portrays, in part 1, a record of my philosophical grounding and development, and in part 2 a record of my efforts to understand the idea of inherent dignity from as many angles as necessary for making intelligible to myself my faith in—and love of—the claim that each person is of incalculable and irreplaceable value.

PART 1

Preliminaries

CHAPTER ONE

Honesty

"Where am I? What does it mean to say: the world? . . . Who am I? How did I get into the world? Why was I not asked about it, why was I not informed of the rules and regulations but just thrust into the ranks [of] human beings? How did I get involved in this big enterprise called actuality? Why should I be involved? . . . And if I am compelled to be involved, where is the manager—I have something to say about this."[1] So writes the Young Man in Søren Kierkegaard's work of "experimental psychology," *Repetition*. The Young Man is asking elementary existential questions. At the center of each of us reside these same questions: Who am I? Where am I? What is actuality? Why am I here? Who is in charge—if anyone?

One can ignore these questions, busying oneself in such a way that they aren't heard. This is a kind of dishonesty, for they are the questions that enable us to face up to what we are—Questioners—and to acknowledge our human situation for what it is. Philosophical honesty begins with paying proper attention to them, and letting them remind us of the givens of existence. Among these givens are the questions themselves—Where am I? What is the world? Should I trust it? Am I loved? They are givens in that I don't decide to ask them; they arise spontaneously. They surge up within my embodied consciousness in a world that is already structured, ordered, the context in which I happen to be happening.

What, most briefly, is this context? Before attempting to respond to this, I should explain that I am employing the word "honesty" (as in, "I should be honest with myself about my existential situation") to mean something slightly different and more precise than merely stating or accepting that such or such is true. Honesty suggests a value beyond mere truth-telling, a value indicated in the sardonic remark of the essayist William Kittredge: "I ask for honesty and what do I get? *Candor*."[2]

Candor is what one can observe watching a tabloid talk show or reality television series: rude exposure of feelings, airing of grievances, brute frankness. Candor is uncensored self-revelation, with caution and tact stripped away, a speaking-forth naked. Most people, most of the time, would prefer—understandably and rightly—to be shielded from candor. Honesty, on the other hand, refers to an action or trait in which there is both truth-telling and *a concern for the recipient*, a respect for how telling or showing or admitting facts will have an effect on, and be beneficial to, the person brought into such confidences. That person, often enough, is oneself: the one to whom one is tactfully and carefully telling the truth, and hoping to help. In other words, being honest is a kind of communicative openness for the purpose of doing good.

It follows that for the person intending to be honest, the degree of openness in revealing what is true will be adapted to the situation. Honesty, for example, doesn't consist in telling a child everything about why the neighbors are getting a divorce. Honesty is not just blurting out facts and feelings. And, especially, it is not self-serving. It cares for the other and for oneself, and it cares about the reality being disclosed. It wants the best for all involved: for the one being honest, for the one learning from honesty, and for the subject matter itself, the truth thus illuminated or confessed. Honesty in philosophical reflections will entail telling the right amount of truth—the amount called for by the context, which in the present case is a specific stage in the development of some extended meditations—and for the right reasons.

When I honestly disclose to myself the particulars of my existential situation, what I manifest is threefold: respect for myself as the one who can discern and disclose, respect for myself as the one who can bear such revelations, and respect for the actuality that I find myself involved in. What are these particulars? Or at least, what are some of the basic particulars? First of all, I am aware that I am participating in something. We can call this something "the process of reality." "Participating" means that I am *of* this process, involved in it and within it. Then, because as a human being I consciously understand some matters, participating humanly means having an intelligent perspective on the process of reality I belong to, but only from within it. I have no access to a standpoint outside the process of reality from which to consider it. Eric Voegelin says that I am not "a self-contained spectator" who can survey reality from a "vantage point outside" of it, from which "its meaning can be viewed."[3] On the contrary, I am an actor *within* reality ("Where am I? Who am I? What is the world?"), and this is what makes suspicious, in fact specious, anyone's claim to know completely or comprehensively what the process of reality is.

Thus I am aware of existing as a conscious participant within a process of reality, as an infinitesimal part of this process, intelligently aware of my personal existence. And I am also aware of the existence of other persons, all of us trying to make sense of what it means to be infinitesimal participants in the unimaginably vast process in which we are occurring. I am also aware, as I participate in the process of reality, that I had nothing to do with deciding to appear in it as a self-aware, intelligent actor: "Why was I not asked about it? Why was I not informed of the rules and regulations but just thrust into the ranks [of] human beings?" No, I had no say in the matter. I am neither the cause of my being here nor the cause of being what I am here, a human creature. In my elementary situation, I am ontologically dependent (or, Kierkegaard would say, a "derived self"), since I am not the cause of my own being.[4] An older philosophical language would say that I am not the kind of being that is a *causa sui* (a "cause of itself," "a self-subsistent cause").

"Cause" here doesn't refer to any of the various senses of worldly cause and effect that might spring to mind. My parents are my *efficient cause*, and in that sense it is they who are the beginning of my existence. One might ask about the *material cause* of my existence, in the sense of what I am made up of, or about my *formal cause* in the sense of what gives my existence its intelligible unity. But the cause under consideration here is that of my ultimate *ontological cause*. My reason concludes that my coming-to-be, like all coming-to-be in the process of reality, must have an ultimate cause or source. So, what is this source?

To put it another way: the whole event of reality, including my existence, raises an inevitable question, an essentially human question: What is the ground of everything, including me? "Where is the manager? I have something to say about this." Furthermore, since the I who I am is my identity in my distinct and unique existence, but ontologically speaking is also my identity with the ground from which I have derived, it seems reasonable to say that I am at once the "I" that individually I am, but also, somehow, the "not I" that is the ground of all being. I cannot help but conclude, in all honesty, that I am an existing finite person who is also, in some way, identical with the ontological cause of my, and all, existence.

CHAPTER TWO

Meaning and Value

As an inquiring and thinking person, I am a conscious participant in the process of reality, a self-aware Question who has some understanding. At the core of my consciousness is a desire to know, which has led, over time, to my wondering who I am, who others are, what reality is, and where everything has come from. Inquiry is the essence of my human mode of participating in reality. There wasn't first a person here (me) discovering itself as a calm and contained self-presence, who subsequently looked around and began to ask, What is all this? Rather, first there was a desire to know, a questioning, an urge to understand (which is both mine as an individual and belongs to the process of reality in which I am participating), which led to my learning more, and more, and eventually to my wondering how I came into existence and what I exist for.

Questioning finds satisfaction in the discovery of meanings and the identification of values, with "values" understood as moral meanings, and meanings understood and affirmed to be genuine "goods." For the present, let "meanings" stand for all that is intelligible, all that has being, and all that is truly good. Through my ongoing, and self-correcting, discovery of many types of meaning—concerning objects, persons, emotions, events, relationships, cause and effect, social practices, tools, institutions, obligations—I have enjoyed (and at times been frightened by) an ever-expanding horizon of understanding. That horizon of understanding is mainly constituted by inherited meanings. Language, both oral and written, the behaviors of others, tools, and much else have conveyed to me an enormous treasure of human insights and ingenuities, and these inherited meanings and values have been supplemented by the results of my efforts to make sense of my own experiences, feelings, encounters, and behavior.

Early on, I came to recognize that my questions about reality extend far beyond my capacities to understand. In fact, in its full scope, my questioning—like all human questioning—intends absolutely all meanings. My desire to know, in other words, is unrestricted. It is a desire to know everything about everything (and, finally, to love everything that is good). Bernard Lonergan remarks that the reason why I don't effectively *will* to know everything about everything is because I discovered soon in life that it is so troublesome to reach even a few answers that the prospect of seeking *all* answers to *all* questions became thoroughly disheartening.[1] Nevertheless, it is because my desire to know is unrestricted that I still wonder, What *is* the whole process of reality?

I find that, from my perspective of participation, I am capable only of some kind of heuristic answer. Whatever reality as a whole is, it is in its totality *the completeness of all intelligible meanings in their being and their value*, all the meanings that have been, are, and will be. When I consider such a completeness of meaning, and wonder about my role in its process, I take into account the fact that being a person (me) has its own peculiar kind of meaning and value. I have been "me" through all the adventures of my personal growth. If a teacher asks me, "What did you do last summer?" he means by "you" the person I have been, am now, and will be as long as I exist, a unity-identity who has developed through time while remaining myself through all my changes and growth.

What kind of meaning and value is this? What happens when I try to explain who I am to a new friend? I tell a story. "Me" is a narrative, a tale, a story open to future developments. As the hero of my own story (as novelists would say), even though I pay attention to my existence and try to guide it through choices based on my memories, knowledge, obligations, and anticipations, I recognize that my personal story is bound up with the stories of other people, that one could tell a larger story, where my story is included in that of, say, my family. The tale of my family is likewise part of an even larger tale, and so on, up to, at the utmost scale of inclusion, a tale that includes the stories of all persons who have ever lived and ever will live—the story of universal humanity.

What is the relationship of this story of universal humanity to the rest of the process of reality, to the aspects of the process that aren't human? Human existence has emerged within the process of reality on the foundations of underlying strata of being: physical, chemical, biological, and animal-sensory levels of being, all of them necessary and integrated components of human existence as we know it. Distinctively human operations, which include self-aware questioning, understanding, knowing, creating, deciding, and loving, depend on and are conditioned (though not fully determined, as my awareness of my use of freedom attests) by these underlying strata of being.[2]

The aspects of the process of reality that aren't human are not therefore alien to human existence. On the contrary, every human being is an integration of elements of all the strata in the observable process of reality. The lower strata "reach into"—and their meanings (and value) are thus implicated in—the meaning of the human existences that have emerged on their basis.[3] The entire process of reality is thus involved in the meaning of the drama of humanity, which is why, in Thomas Mann's words, "with the world-whole and its unity the human being has always and ever to do, whether he knows it or not."[4]

But what is this meaning and value of the world-whole, on which the meaning and value of my story, my minuscule role, depend? Again, no one can know substantive (as distinct from heuristic) answers to this, given the human perspective from participation within the process of reality. Who am I? Where am I? All answers to these questions recede into realms of meaning that we know to be mysteries to us. Each of us is thus inescapably *involved in mystery*: the mystery of the meaning of the universal human drama, which is bound up with the mystery of the meaning of the entire process of reality. Voegelin sums up the matter this way: "The Mystery of the historical process is inseparable from the Mystery of a reality that brings forth the universe and the earth, plant and animal life on earth, and ultimately man and his consciousness."[5]

Each of us can grasp that the totality of what has been, is, and will come to pass—the Whole includes the entirety of meanings, which is a narrative completeness. The fact that the process in which we are involved is evolving, that it is a dynamic unfolding in the process of development, doesn't alter the fact that the Whole we conceive of embraces *all* meanings and values, including those that, from our perspective, belong to the future. Our human awareness of being participants in a *narrative completeness of meaning and value*, that is, a story that includes its not-yet-arrived-at fulfilment, has given rise in some cultures to eschatological yearning and sentiment: an anticipation of, and desire to know about, contribute to, and participate in, an imagined conclusion of the story of existence and reality.

One measure of honesty about our situation as questioners aware of being actors in a story that is a narrative completeness of meaning, is to recognize the intelligibility of this eschatological longing. If one fails to grasp this particular intelligibility as meaningful, as one of the meanings apprehended in the immense human effort to make sense of existence and history, one will have placed oneself at a philosophical disadvantage.

CHAPTER THREE

The Cosmos

The whole of reality, if one includes past, present, and future, is the narrative completeness of meaning in which each of us is participating. This whole needs a name. It can be called *the cosmos*. The idea that the cosmos divides into two distinct realms of meaning, immanent and transcendent, is a fairly recent accomplishment of human consciousness. It entered human thinking and teaching from radical experiences and insights occurring during the first millennium BCE, in the cultures of ancient Israel, classical Greece, Zoroastrian Persia, the region of the Indian subcontinent, and the China of Confucius and Laozi (Lao-Tse). In all human cultures before that (and in many concurrently and afterward), the unified whole of reality, the cosmos, was felt and understood in what may be called a "compact" way, in which, on the one hand, sacred forces, and on the other, the natural world were perceived and felt to be interfused, interpenetrating, and patterned after one other. In compact consciousness, divine reality is palpable in physical things, especially celestial objects and nature's forces, human society is founded in and imitates divine society, plants and animals participate in sacred being, and gods can become persons and persons gods. Metamorphoses and transformations are continual. The objects and energies of the cosmos, in brief, have a certain permeability for each other. Thus, the process of reality is experienced in compact consciousness as a "charmed community," where divine origins and all other beings are felt to share a basic substance, are experienced as (to use a technical term) consubstantial.[1]

The cosmos of compact consciousness has a certain stability, which consists of the enduring consubstantial rhythms of cycles—divine, celestial, natural, social, and personal. The narrative completeness that is the cosmos of past, present, and future meanings is conceived in terms of endless cyclicality. There is as yet no thought of a final, spiritual exodus of world or persons out of the cycling structures of the cosmos into an eschatological "after" or "beyond."

Once, however, it has been discovered and successfully taught that divine or sacred reality consists of an *absolutely transcendent* meaning (i.e., that the divine essence transcends both space and time, and also transcends human perception and imagination, conceptual understanding, and language), human thinking tends toward differentiating the wholeness of meaning into two distinct realms or dimensions. This differentiation of the cosmos, it is important to remember, is a matter of human insights: *it takes place only within consciousness.* Voegelin: "There is no Beyond lying around somewhere[;] there is no differentiated insight concerning [transcendence] and its presence in the cosmos at all, as long as there is no experience of [its] presence in the act of meditation."[2]

At the same time, the oneness of the cosmos remains the permanent presupposition of any differentiating discovery of a transcendent Beyond. The latter discovery does not cancel out the former fact. The human mind, participating in a Whole, merely differentiates realms of meaning within the Whole (the cosmos) in which it is participating. Compact consciousness was already aware of transcendent Mystery: its stories and rituals portray the gods and their ways as mostly unknowable. Sometimes in early myth there is an utmost god behind the other gods whose reality is impossible to ascertain, sometimes there is a Hidden God, a Primal God of pure light, an uncreated Ultimate, and so on. What the first millennium BCE breakthroughs presented was the *explicit identification and defining* of an absolutely transcendent realm of divine, or primal, meaning, with the rational paradoxes of its articulation appreciated as such, a radical Mystery that led, in time, to the delegitimization of the gods of early myth, or at least to their demotion to symbolic intermediaries, or to some other kind of spiritual-creative circuitry within cosmic process, such as the psychic forces of Jungian and other "depth" psychologies.

But here is the problematic thing for appreciation of the cosmos: gradually, after the differentiation of an absolutely transcendent realm of meaning has taken place and radiated sufficiently through world cultures, the oneness of reality starts to become elusive. One reason for this elusiveness is the deep temptation for human imagination to separate the differentiated realms of meaning—immanence and transcendence—into two discontinuous realities, one "here" and one "out there." This misleading spatializing of realms of meaning seems to be almost unavoidable because of the human need to try to visualize whatever we think of as real. But absolute transcendence is not about space, or place; it is not discovered in the way that new lands are found. Rather, it is revealed through the meditative discovery that the ultimate ground of the process of reality sought by human questioning, and the perfect goodness sought by moral longing and love (this ultimate ground and perfect goodness being identical), are not known by meanings intrinsic to the universe of space and time.

Another reason that the unity of the cosmos becomes elusive after the discovery of radical transcendence is that once vision splits the cosmos into two realms of meaning, transcendent reality is looked for quite unsuccessfully by those who wish to confirm it in some empirical manner, as if it were a thing like other things, with the unsurprising result that, since it cannot be empirically confirmed, it is pronounced to be illusory. And so a countervision emerges in which the only reality is the immanent world: the spatiotemporal universe. The cosmos—that is, the universe *plus* the radical divine Mystery of its ground—is lost from view, as the disenchanted world by itself is embraced as the totality of being. It is forgotten, or ignored, that the notions of immanence and transcendence only make conceptual sense as a linked unity, that "immanent reality" is no more intelligible as a notion apart from that of "transcendent reality" than the notion of good is intelligible apart from the notion of bad, or the notion of light is intelligible apart from the notion of dark. Thus it is that the cosmos is conceptually and imaginatively replaced by the spatiotemporal universe.

One consequence of this is that the narrative completeness of meaning itself is discredited. For without my story and the universal human story being grounded in an *ultimate* story, in relation to which the dynamic evolution of the universe (including human emergence) finds a sufficient cause and orienting purpose—the key word here being "sufficient," meaning capable, in principle, of accounting for *all* cosmic and human phenomena, including our eschatological yearnings—the search for a deep sense to personal and historical stories fades into silence and embarrassment, amid accusations of wishing to believe in fairy tales.

This situation is not one of being lost in the cosmos. It is that of having lost the cosmos. What does remembering the cosmos entail? First of all, accepting that there is a Mystery of transcendent meaning that constitutes the grounding "plus" of reality.

CHAPTER FOUR

Belonging

As a human being, I know that I am a derived reality, that I am not self-caused. I am not the ground of my own being. So what is? "We are stardust," sings Joni Mitchell. Well, yes. But where did stardust come from? It is somewhat customary and somewhat pleasing (at least for some people I know) to stop at stardust: at the primal energy-matter that swirls and blazes and expands in the impossibly immense universe (light travels nearly 6 trillion miles a year, and the diameter of the observable universe is about 93 billion light-years), that coalesces in chemical elements and compounds, that in a breathtaking sequence of dynamic emergences has integrated itself "upward" on planet Earth (and who knows, in what parallel fashion, elsewhere), into sea and atmosphere, primitive life, plants, animals, and ourselves.

But questioning—left to its own devices—refuses to stop at energy-matter. It asks, What is the cause of stardust? It won't do to say, "Nothing." And it won't do to respond with, "That's a foolish question." The question always reasserts itself—it "nibbles at the soul," Emily Dickinson says.[1] It does so because, although it consistently leads questioning to a boundary where the human mind confronts the failures of its own powers of understanding, it is not an unreasonable question.

In fact, there is no reason to consider reason itself to be trustworthy (a trust that performatively is the very guidance of everyday existing) unless its built-in, spontaneous curiosity about the ultimate origin of every cause—about the ground of the narrative completeness of meaning—is accepted as a proper, good, and rational question. Reason, in light of this natural terminus of the questioning that has propelled it from the start, *is* openness of inquiry to the ground of its own occurrence, its own being.

Consequently, I ask (as everyone who has lived long enough asks), To what do I belong, in an ultimate sense? To the cosmos, yes. But the cosmos is the process of reality in the completeness of its meanings. Since we know that we can't know in any substantial manner this completeness, this whole, because human existing and knowing are a participation within it, but still we know *of* the whole and reasonably ask about its ultimate ground, let us consider the ground of the process of reality to be a heuristically anticipated origin of all meanings, including the meanings of the complete stories of all human existences.

More fundamentally than to all else that we belong to, we belong to *that*—whatever the ground is. This could seem like a sudden leap into the furthest reaches of abstraction. Since these reflections about my existence are being guided with an eye toward the topic of inherent human dignity, shouldn't I concern myself with the much more obvious and immediate fact that I *belong to myself*? After all, human cultural developments have made inescapable the serious, inspiring, and frightening truth that each of us is in our own care, is responsible for making of ourselves what we should, has an obligation to take charge, to the degree possible, of the life story each of us has been granted. We rightly recognize that the springboard for authentic living is the recognition that one belongs to oneself (a trauma for adolescence!) and that one can't in good conscience offload the job of managing one's existence onto anyone else, such as the crowd, parents, friends, history, or the anonymous social power that Heidegger calls "the they."[2]

It is true, of course, that this belonging-to-and-responsibility-for-self happens in a situation full of givens. Existence is bodily located, and my body (with its imperatives and impulses) exists within a family, a community, language(s), traditions, all of which affect and inform my self-management, and which from beginning to end entail dialogues (sometimes conscious and sometimes not) wherein I learn and test, attempt, backtrack, blunder into (or create) new situations, situations to which my continually altering self-understanding must adapt.

But still, for all this situatedness and intersubjective becoming, I *do* belong to myself, in a way that I can't escape. Sartre says, with a sour smirk, I am condemned to be free.[3] Then again, at the same time, I can't help being aware that my being given to myself for self-management was not my own doing. I can shape myself, freely determine this or that about myself or alter this or that about my situational circumstances, because I have been *granted* that freedom. And because I have indeed been (Heidegger says) "thrown into being," I spontaneously ask, What or who did the throwing? That is the question of the ground. And to this mysterious ground I most fundamentally belong, in the sense that to it I owe everything—that is, myself.[4]

So when I ask myself how I am to shape myself, the question is permeated by a sense of responsibility to that from which I have ultimately derived. If I am existentially honest, I find that I owe it to myself to be "true to"—to live in accordance with, to be attuned to—the ground of my existence. In other words, to properly claim myself, I need to do my best to unify myself with the origin and essence of all things, by continually adjusting in appropriate ways my conscious participation in the cosmos. The major philosophical and religious traditions all agree on this point. How should one live? In accordance with the Tao. Or, in growing existential response to the recognition that my deepest self, *atman*, is identical with the one transcendent reality, *Brahman* (the central teaching of the Hindu *Upanishads*). Or, one should speak and act in harmony with the *Logos* (Heraclitus, Plato). Or, the Hebrew prophet Micah writes that we should seek justice, practice kindness, and walk humbly with our God (Mic. 6:8).

But what if these traditional words and symbols meant to orient us just seem so old, so disconnected with the present, that as they reach our minds, they are dead on arrival, hollow-sounding, sound without sense? Then, a person will have to try to grow into authentic value and virtue on the basis of moral instructions, advice, and sayings tossed up by present-day culture, most of them at odds with each other, and many of them, contrary to the wisdom traditions just mentioned, reflecting the supposition that the immanent universe is the whole of reality. Indeed, the rejection of any transcendent realm of meaning is one of the hallmarks of modernity. "The civilization of the current age ever more spectacularly tries to arrange its affairs while refuting all forms of transcendence," and in multitudinous modern voices "registers the renunciation of transcendence as a victory," writes László Földényi.[5]

Still, a sensitive and discerning consciousness—one not lazily indifferent to the rational impasse of immanentism, and not in thrall to fads or ideologies that channel ultimate concern toward idols of science, technology, wealth, social power, pleasures, or self-esteem—will suspect that, for itself, the (transcendent) Measure has yet to be found. And if skepticism about current fads and modern ideologies keeps one searching, and if disgust with the existential ineptitude of those who manifest a closed-minded obeisance to religious authority doesn't prompt one on principle to abandon the search for a genuine cosmic ground, then honest efforts to remember the Mystery to which one ultimately belongs will recur. If they do recur, it may become apparent that acknowledging that one's existence belongs originally to a transcendent "all-humbling darkness" (Dylan Thomas) is a kind of . . . courtesy.[6]

"Courtesy" might be defined as "a respect desiring to be helpful." Courtesy toward our own utmost origins wants to help it show itself in our doings. The ground of the process of reality does not depend upon our efforts, since it is self-sufficient, overflowing, and creative. But our courtesy toward it *glorifies* it, while bringing our own lives into a certain stability of witness. We don't get to comprehend the truth at the center of the narrative completeness of meaning, but we get to acknowledge that there are acts of remembrance we can perform in which we grant that what we most deeply belong to is the ultimate freedom that gave us our freedom, and that through these acts of remembrance we come to belong to ourselves in a remarkably clarifying way.

These are also the acts—one traditional name for them is "love"—through which we come to belong, properly speaking, to another person, or to numerous others through social or political friendship. For persons can belong to each other only by way of belonging to the shared ground of their existences. T. S. Eliot noted, with sadness, that many are paralyzed by a fear "of belonging to another, or to others, or to God."[7]

It is of course a paradoxical kind of courtesy that accepts that we come to ourselves and belong to ourselves only by recognizing and feeling that we don't ultimately belong to ourselves: that a person discovers the essence of their unique, participating personhood only by realizing an identity with the mysterious ground of all reality. But it remains a paradoxical rule that greater individuation requires deepening communion, and that deepening communion leads to greater individuation. One becomes more the self of one's destiny by continually losing oneself in deepening identity with what is. A. P. Gütersloh says, "Die Tiefe ist aussen" (Depth is discovered outward).[8]

What is the goal of this development, this being a tuning fork that vibrates with recurrent remembrance of the transcendent source of personal identity? It appears to be to learn how better to act with loving courtesy toward the Whole, which, in its immanent realm of meaning, as the world proportionate to finite human knowing, continues to emerge in dynamic glory from the ground of the process of reality. We can recognize exemplary models of this learning in certain famous individuals in history, and also sometimes in the news, and, if we are very fortunate, in personal life—those who have "developed well." Every especially loving person is a transparency for the Measure from which we all have derived, a person who invites us to actualize our own possibilities of similar transparency. How much we measure up will in the end have to do with how well we manage to belong to ourselves by belonging to our source.

CHAPTER FIVE

The Desire to Know

We can belong to ourselves, and the cosmos, *and* the ground of being, because we have emerged in a situation. Bodily I was conceived, bodily I gestated, bodily I came from the womb, timed and placed. Insofar as I am a bodily being, I am in physical continuity with the world, and a discrete entity within it. Because human existence is bodily and situated, some high thinkers (and low) draw the conclusion that an individual's behavior is completely determined. They contend that if one could know all the causal effects on an individual of all material elements, from nucleotides to tidal pulls, one could infallibly predict every behavioral act, thought, and utterance of a human being from womb to tomb.

But reflecting on my existing, I cannot escape what presents itself as a rather obvious fact: that as humans develop, freedom—freedom to attend to this rather than to that, freedom to stop and reflect or not, freedom to choose this instead of that course of action (and the freedom to accept responsibility for one's intentions and behaviors)—comes to inform, to some degree, each personal drama. It dawns on me, at some point along the path of my development, that it is up to me to set about crafting or shaping myself: that my life story is not simply determined, not only fated through inexorable givens, but also self-guided to some degree, which means that to some degree it is *spiritually* (not merely materially or physically, but freely) guided. What should we call this human condition of "fate plus freedom"? Martin Buber calls it *meaning*, and also *destiny*.[1]

But how does it happen, this freedom? Not in the sense of, What is its ultimate source (the unimaginable Freedom from which all situated human freedom is derived)? Rather, What is the *phenomenon* of freedom in me, the freedom that when exercised is—one might say—in its intending and acting the crucial and utmost me? The human exercise of freedom always involves at least some degree of understanding. So here is one way to think about the situatedness of freedom—as a phenomenon occurring along with the presence of certain other physical and psychological phenomena.

A human being is an intricately complex mixture of many situated desires. Still, among all of them one can differentiate a conscious (that is, a self-aware) desire to understand and to know: a longing to make sense of things while we are conscious that we are doing so. This is a human-only desire, distinct from those experienced by animals, no matter how sophisticated the animal psychology. The key to this human difference is that the human desire to know unfolds as *self-aware* inquiry, and acts of understanding, and a seeking to confirm that one's ideas are grounded in reality independent of one's thinking, and a knowing that objects truly exist apart from one's thinking about them—with the term "self-aware" here, crucially, referring to the fact that these mental operations are accompanied by an awareness of the objects to be known *and* by an awareness of the self that is performing these operations. This is an awareness *of* being aware, first, that one exists (which is why Heidegger calls humanness *Dasein*, "to-be-there"), and second, that one is desiring to know and coming to know.[2]

It is because of this desire—the desire to understand and know—operating among all our other desires, that we are persons, and that we have a personal story and know that we have one, and also that we know that we participate in a universal human story. There is no evidence that dogs understand they are participating in a universal dog story. Supposing there to be a universal dog story.

Of course, as humans, we want to feel deeply, to be joyful, to grieve, to be in dialogue, to have adventures, to be creative, to be ecstatic, to explore what our sensations have to offer, to eat the best food and drink the best drinks, to dream. But all of these are done humanly only if and when they are accompanied (in the moment or afterward) by at least some measure of self-aware understanding. Even a descent into "mindless" Dionysian frenzy is humanly interesting only because for its duration emotion is drenched with a sense of meaningfulness and because its meanings can (to a degree) be parsed by later understanding.

One might say, therefore, that the human *métier* is consciously (i.e., with self-awareness) seeking, discovering, and creating meanings. As meanings accumulate for each of us, they make up a personal horizon of understanding. And as everyone knows, the more meanings one comes to understand, the more meanings one recognizes to be beyond one's present horizon of understanding. At our core, what we want is to understand everything about everything: we want to comprehend what this Whole is in which we are participating (even though we are incapable of attaining that end), because after all, only through knowing the meaning of the Whole could one know the meaning of one's own story.

From within my consciousness—that is, speaking psychologically—I experience my desire-to-know-meaning as one desire among others. But what is it ontologically? What kind of *being* is this seeking-for-meaning? Careful reflection shows that it is the actualizing of a human potentiality to *become* whatever the mind grasps through understanding—and "become" here is not a metaphor. My mind ontologically becomes that which it understands, a fact about human cognition first systematically explained by Aristotle.[3] This doesn't mean that by understanding what a bicycle is I become a bicycle, or that by recognizing that an act is courageous, I become that act, or become courageous. It means something more ontologically restricted, but still of considerable importance for grasping how the human mind operates. Aristotle put the matter this way: "intelligence in act" and "the intelligible in act" are identical, are one and the same.[4] Why must this be so?

First, an object understood (be it a tree that one sees, or a deed that one witnesses, or an emotion that one feels), to the degree that it *is* understood, is an *intelligible meaning* (e.g., of a thing, attribute, distinction, relationship, circumstance, choice, value, possibility, probability, event, confluence of events, "chaos" of improbabilities, absurdity). Second, what a mind comes to "possess" through insight is that same intelligible meaning. Third, this intelligible meaning (or "form," as Plato, Aristotle, and Aquinas called it) is identical in the understanding (mind) and in the object understood. It doesn't matter what the meaning is that the mind understands; whatever it is, the mind becomes it *as intelligibility*, and in that act, the potential of the mind to become this particular meaning is made actual. All the meanings that I become in this way exist independently of my mind except, of course, for those that don't, such as ungrounded hypotheses, misinterpretations, hallucinations, and delusions, which exist only as objects "of" my mind.

What makes it difficult to accept that a human mind is "able to become all things" (Aristotle) through grasping meanings is the propensity of most people (including some influential philosophers) to imagine that the mind that is inquiring, on the one hand, and whatever objects this mind might be inquiring about, on the other, are confronting each other precisely like physical objects in space. My inquiring and understanding mind is imagined to be "in here" (somewhere in the head, in the brain), and everything else is imagined to be "out there"—or, with regard to objects of inquiry that are somehow also "inside" me, such as emotions and ideas, as being also "in here" along with, or in, the mind. All this sort of thinking is based on the presumption that everything real, mind included, is a spatial or material object.

But the mind's acts of understanding—of grasping meaning—are acts of personhood, and as such are not a material process or action, even though they depend on and are conditioned by the functioning of underlying material manifolds; they are an actualizing of spiritual reality, that is, an actualizing of a nonphysical reality.

"Spirit" in this sense (and there is another, more restrictive meaning of "spirit," referring to certain high achievements of the self that are made possible by the self's participation in the freedom of the transcendent ground, but we are using the term here to refer merely to the nonphysical nature of human conscious operations) is primarily what is meant when I refer to my "self." For by "self," I typically mean "character," which cannot be sketched on paper because it is invisible—a spiritual, not a physical, reality. Or, explaining who my friend is, it is his personality, not for example his height and weight, that I think of as essentially "him." What am I, then? As a human, I am an individual who is a bodily-and-socially-and-environmentally-situated-spirit.

This unity of "situated spirit" must not be understood in a Cartesian fashion, as a nonphysical substance inexplicably attached to a machine-like body-substance. All the levels of being involved in existence are intelligibly united through each lower manifold (starting with the subatomic) being organized by a sequence of higher integrating processes (chemical, biological, animal-perceptual), culminating in the nonphysical operations of mind that integrate them, while still ontologically depending upon and being conditioned by them. A human being is thus a *unity* of all its levels of being, even if by "self" we primarily refer to the fruit of a person's cumulative mental propensities, habits, and operations, which are not themselves intrinsically physical. The upsurging of myself as situated spirit, as I always need to remind myself, was not of my own doing: my personhood is also the ground of being itself emerging as my existence within the process of reality.

Spirit as individual is seeking to become—through understanding and knowing and loving—whatever is, and, insofar as it wants to exist harmoniously and knowingly with its own ground, to attune itself to its own ultimate source. This seeking, needless to say, can get sidetracked. Wayward desires can bear me away from the freedom of personal self-determining. We might define as "wayward" all those desires that succeed in bearing me away from personhood. More precisely, there are desires that I *allow* to carry me away from understanding, knowing, deciding well, and loving. In which case my bodily-and-socially-and-environmentally-situated spiritual existence as a whole . . . wanders off.

CHAPTER SIX

Myth

With our unrestricted desire to make sense of experience, we humans—bodily, situated, spiritual—find ourselves presented with a staggering challenge: to figure out what this cosmos is that we are participating in. Or to figure out as much of it as we can. And why we are participating. And what we are supposed to do, on the basis of what we have come to know. And to do all this honestly, that is, with as little self-deception as possible, respectfully, and with a readiness both to accept that some former judgments have been mistakes and to try to correct them.

In order to take up this task in our particular individual ways, whoever we are and however we've been situated, we have to gather what's going on from all the clues that the cosmos has on offer. Those clues include what has been done, spoken, and written by persons as a result of extraordinary experiences of identity and communion with the ground of being in which we participate: actions, sayings, and writings viewed as inspired or revelatory. How can we absorb the meaning of those kinds of clues? We will be helped if we try to explore, briefly, our situation through ancient eyes, imagining how matters looked to early humans, and then return to the theme of radical transcendence.

Why, it was asked by all ancients, are things the way they are? Why does the sun rise and move across the sky? How does rain make plants grow? What is the source of a toothache? The answers must lie most basically, it seemed obvious, in those powers beyond us (after all, we didn't set these matters in motion), which are ultimately responsible for the ordering of things, and are regarded as sacred for just that reason, namely, gods and goddesses, and everything else that is a source of sacred power and intent. It would be natural to think that we'd better align ourselves with these powers. Not merely so as not to suffer from "the displeasure of the gods," but above all for society and human activity to be in harmony with the way the cosmos is, to be "well-ordered" through being rightly attuned with the powers revealed in the cosmos.

Our human desire to know requires us to think and communicate to others about these matters in which we are intimately involved. And the language expressing understanding of such existential intimacies is that of *symbols*, or complexes of images (including words), enacted and uttered, that well up from our rootedness in the cosmos, images infused with and haunted by deep emotions. These symbols are retained and accumulated and preserved and venerated when they are convincing in their expression about what it means to exist in the cosmic process. And so we gesture or dance or daub or construct or sing or speak these symbols, again and again.

The earliest symbols of song, dance, and picture eventually became elaborate tales. And the tales were gathered so as to construct inspiring and comforting shelters of culture. They satisfied the felt understanding (such as it has been) as to what this awesome, terrifying, joyful, sorrowful journey of participating in the cosmos appears to be about. Venerated cosmic symbols and tales were felt to have sprung *necessarily* from the sacred depths of the cosmos itself (from the united "community of being," to use Eric Voegelin's expression[1]), because—as we would put it now—to be human is to have a story that is part of the cosmic story, and it is inconceivable, to curious and worshipping humans, that the cosmos would not reveal its own Tale. Thus, certain symbols and tales were embraced as the essential cosmos-revealed and cosmos-interpreting *myths* (Gr. *mythoi*; plural of *mythos* = "report," "tale," "story").

Because ancient myths wove, out of innumerable factors, fabrics that convincingly communicated the meaning, order, and value of the cosmos for human societies, and enabled their members to find meaning-making adjustment within it, they functioned as a foundational "style of truth" (Voegelin).[2] Ancient myths revealed for their listeners truths of the human situation, and in them experiences of cyclical (repeatable) aspects of existence in time received more emphasis than experiences of linear (unrepeatable) aspects of existence in time.

Ancient, or what might be called "cosmological," myth proved, however, to be an inherently vulnerable and unstable style of truth, which seems odd, given that this was the manner in which persons from original human times had made the cosmos understandable to themselves. But as history has shown, cosmological myth was susceptible to being undermined, eroded, and in the end dismissed as not being the most convincing style of truth for illuminating the order of the cosmos and the purposes of human existence.

What was it that exposed the vulnerabilities of ancient myths, finally weakening their power to convince and to console? It was the differentiations between "world-of-things-in-space-and-time" and "world-transcending-ground-of-being," which began to appear during the first millennium BCE in diverse cultures and different languages, and that unfolded their meanings over centuries. Everywhere the differentiating teachings spread (and they did so with varying degrees of rapidity and thoroughness), they were destructive of the style of truth of ancient or cosmological myth, because now, divinity or ultimacy—the essence of beyond-human powers—had been found to be *radically other* than celestial objects, worldly processes, forces, places, animals, kings. The disempowering of gods and goddesses had begun, or, in whatever fashion these did remain potent in the religious imaginations and practices of peoples, they gradually became suspected (or accused) of being only transparencies for an invisible, transcendent ground of being "beyond" the world.

This is not to deny that, in contemporary times, this mountain, this grove of trees, this desert canyon, the orb of our moon, can feel sacred to you. But even if so, this is not the same sense of the immediate and absolutely sacred nature of such objects as felt by ancient peoples, because all of us have been made conscious, like it or not, of the fact that if there is indeed an ultimate sacred reality, or realm of meaning, it is utterly placeless and timeless. In other words, the differentiation of the ground of reality as radically transcendent disturbed everything. The myths that were once the cosmos telling the cyclical truth of its Tale became mere legends, paintings, figures, dreams, and, finally in the last of their demotions, became tourism for those wanting to feel connected to a recondite enchantment.

The waning of the power of cosmological myth did not, however, render myth itself obsolescent: still powerful were myths understood as symbols and tales that truly mediate the meaning of the Tale of the cosmos and the meaning of human existence. Myths remained crucial, because human beings, to feel that their lives are meaningful, have always needed symbols and tales that illuminate and guide their relationship with the transcendent Mystery of the ground in whose power they originated, and with whose perfection and radiating meaning humans long to exist in harmony.

Thus, the drawn-out experiences wherein transcendent reality was discovered and revealed gave birth to new kinds of religious myths, myths that tell stories about human souls explicitly participating in radical transcendence. These are stories of cosmos and humanity that describe the peregrinations and purposes of self-aware, knowing, and at their best loving beings who consciously (whether or not they admit it to themselves) are simultaneously participating in the world and a "beyond" of the world. They are the differentiated religious myths that are the heart of late Hinduism and of Buddhism, and also of Judaism, Christianity, and Islam, the Religions of the Book, in whose myths experiences of linear (unrepeatable) aspects of existence in time receive more emphasis than experiences of cyclical (repeatable) aspects of existence in time, that is, which are essentially eschatological.

All differentiated religious myths are understood, of course, to be grounded in extraordinary human experiences of identity and communion with the ground of being. That is, the transcendent ground of reality itself is understood to be speaking in and through them. But for many in modernity (though they are a minority of the globe's population), these differentiated religious myths have in turn lost their convincingness, so that some moderns are mythless. The truly mythless, though, are a tiny fraction of people, because most people who feel alien to both cosmological and differentiated religious myths still believe in a host of *secular* myths. For myths can function precisely as myths—as symbolic complexes suggesting ultimate or cosmic meaning—in secular modes of attention and concern, such as art and politics.

During the last two centuries, artists have been most perspicacious in recognizing and attempting to satisfy a need for mythic symbols that convey a fresh sense of transcendent meaning for the secular-minded: consider the writings of Blake and Emily Dickinson, the aspirations of the Romantics, Wagner's Ring Cycle and Mahler's symphonies, Joyce's *Ulysses*, the paintings of Kandinsky or Rothko. Or consider rock 'n' roll. Antonin Artaud was supremely clear about what the art of theater ought to do in the twentieth century: "Theatre's true purpose is to create Myths, to express life from an immense, universal aspect and to deduce imagery from this life where we would like to discover ourselves."[3]

But in the twentieth century it was film, above all, that stepped in to mythically orientate, in a secular mode, existence in the cosmos, for better or worse. Some view the influence of film in this particular respect to have mostly been destructive; the historian Friedrich Heer once stated that film, especially in its later incarnation as sound film, "has killed more people than the machine-gun."[4]

"Political myths," about which much has been written in recent times, is a topic we will return to. For now, let us only note that one widely embraced political *mythos* in our times is that of equal inherent human dignity.

CHAPTER SEVEN

The World of Space and Time

Discovery of the radical transcendence of ultimate reality—whether understood as Tao, Brahman, *Logos*, Yahweh, the Trinitarian God, or Allah—alters how the world, initially experienced as the showing-forth of the completeness of the cosmos, comes to be apprehended. In short, it becomes a spatiotemporal universe. It becomes, slowly and inevitably, if often incompletely, de-divinized. The one cosmos, the Whole, conceptually splits into worldly being and transcendent being. Immediate divine identity dissolves out of worldly things: out of the sun and moon and stars, sky and sea, storms and winds, mountains and rivers, birds and other animals, divine kings and Pharaohs. This is the differentiation (the distinguishing between conceptually separable realms of meaning within the cosmos) that eventually invites a disinterested analysis of what will come to be called in Western culture "nature."

The word "nature" of course has many meanings. One might speak of the "nature of something," meaning its essence. Or one might use the term to refer to the biological realm. The word in fact has dozens of meanings. But we are able to use the term "nature" also to signify "the entirety of the spatiotemporal universe" because that universe, after the discovery of transcendent reality, is conceptually approachable as its own order of being, distinct from immediate divine presence. "Nature," in other words, has become an autonomous realm of meaning.[1]

As a consequence, nature (the spatiotemporal universe) is now subject to being investigated on its own terms, that is, in terms of the intrinsic intelligibilities (intrinsic meanings) of things. For example, one seeks to understand the inherent properties and attributes of physical objects, or the developmental laws or tendencies inherent in biological things, or the recurrently causal interdependent relationships between objects in nature.

With regard to the sphere of human beings and their activities of social self-organization, there arises the issue of the nature—especially, of the proper character—of social or political orders conceived independently of divine founding, or of divinity as manifest immediately in leaders, or of divinity as dictating the laws that guide human affairs. Just as "physics" is now conceivable as an independently understood region of meanings, so too is "politics." But still, in such examining, where intelligible aspects of the world are explored without reference to immediate divine presence, is the world thereby genuinely sundered from the transcendent ground of its being, from divine, or ultimate, reality?

In the language of Western religious traditions, Is the world actually severed from God? In the language of classical Chinese thought, Is the world actually severed from the Tao? Not at all. The cosmos is still one; it remains a unity. But because that is so, the intimacy between radically transcendent reality and everything else—the relationship between God and all else, or between the Tao and all else, or between Brahman and all else—is formidably complicated to think through. *How* is the transcendent present in the immanent, the natural? In what manner does the natural thing, the worldly, depend for its being and its meaning on the transcendent? This is the problem set for everyone who comes to the cultural table after the differentiation of world and transcendent reality. It is a problem whose burden remains with us.

In considering it, what should first of all be remembered is that the *conceptual autonomy* granted to the de-divinized world of space and time, as a result of distinguishing out from it a transcendent ground of reality—whether transcendence is regarded as an impersonal principle, such as the Chinese Tao, or as a personal divinity, such as the Jewish and Christian Creator-God—is only a *relative* autonomy. Discovering the radical transcendence of ultimate reality does not dissolve the intimate relationship between the order of things in the world and the ordering transcendent ground sustaining them. The permanent danger for thought that inheres in the articulation of any notion of transcendent reality is that its "beyondness" will be imagined to be some kind of spatially separate thing: "world" here, God (or Tao) "out there."

This is why it is helpful (following Lonergan) to refer to transcendent reality as a *realm of meaning*, a realm that, though distinguishable from other realms of meaning, must not be conceived as an "elsewhere," or as any kind of entity apart from the world. We make a massive blunder if we forget that our foundational experience of reality is always that of the cosmos, of participating in a completeness of meaning, the completeness of the process of reality, including its ground.

Remembering the cosmos, we recognize that, Voegelin says, "there are no things that are merely immanent," since our primary experience of reality is that of its wholeness.[2] The conceptual splitting of reality into the two realms of transcendent and immanent meaning makes for stupefying intellectual difficulties, as attested by the historical record of efforts East and West to articulate the intelligible relationship between these two realms. It also presents peculiar challenges for understanding what constitutes a proper existential comportment toward a reality composed of "world plus transcendence." But foundationally, any interpretatively sound (if always imperfect) response to these difficulties and challenges is impossible if we misunderstand transcendent reality to be some type of thing apart from "nature."

Recognizing this misunderstanding to be the blunder that it is has given rise, in the treatment of ultimate matters, to such locutions of paradox-in-language that we find, for example, in a text such as the Buddhist *Heart Sutra* (likely composed in the first century CE). We learn here that if transcendent reality is not a thing, then it is "no-thing," it is nothing. But it is not *nothing* in the sense of being non-real, meaningless, and or irrelevant. It is the deeper reality of worldly things. So (the sutra reveals) if one penetrates any natural "form" thoroughly enough, one experiences it as identical with transcendent "emptiness." Therefore the *Heart Sutra* (as translated by Red Pine): "Form is emptiness, emptiness is form; / emptiness is not separate from form, / form is not separate from emptiness; / whatever is form is emptiness, / whatever is emptiness is form."[3]

Language is always foundering here. Things of the world are constantly changing, and they perish. How are we to properly apprehend their relationship with the transcendent "nothing" or "emptiness" that is their origination and sustenance, and that does not change or perish, and that somehow—but not simply—is identical with the world of things? To make sense of the text of the *Heart Sutra* is to recognize how difficult it is not to wander offtrack in thinking through the transcendence/immanence relationship.

There are comparative difficulties in Western religious teachings. How are we meant to understand the relationship between things of the natural world and their transcendently personal Creator-God? This is one of the central questions explored by Western mystics. Here we find such formulations as "God is everywhere and nowhere," formulations intended to prompt the realization that God is not an entity, that descriptions derived from sense-based experiences of spatiotemporal things don't apply to radical divine transcendence, that "transcendence" is, Voegelin says, an "exegetic, not *descriptive*" term.[4]

Understanding that any word such as "transcendence" is not a description of anything that we can sensorily experience, but understanding at the same time that human knowing always relies on descriptive images to direct the human search for insights into nondescribable realities, wisdom teachers and mystics have found many ways to employ descriptive language to convey to readers that this language itself must be "gone beyond" if one is to rightly understand the relationship between transcendence and world. Poets too, of course, and other writers have exploited descriptive images to indicate that the transcendent realm of meaning transcends language and to provoke appropriate insights into the transcendence/immanence relationship. For instance, the fifteenth-century Islamic mystic Kabir, who was influenced by Sufi poets and by Hindu teachings, writes (in Robert Bly's version): "Student, tell me what is God? He is the breath inside the breath."[5] This is not a conceptual explanation. It is an image, a symbol, of ultimate intimacy. It may be dismissed as meaningless if one wants a logical account of ultimate things. But Kabir, as do poets in all differentiated religious traditions, would insist that one can have experiences and insights that make "He is the breath inside the breath" a meaningful, cosmos-and-existence-illuminating, phrase.

The key to all this is to understand that Kabir's is not a phrase about things, but it rather points to experiences in which a certain kind of relationship within the cosmos is revealed, experiences that lead to the insight that there are no things that are merely immanent, and that one's own existence is continually grounded in transcendent reality. Within the major differentiating traditions of East and West, there was something unique—as historical developments came to prove—about the way classical Greek philosophers encountered and articulated divine transcendence. For Parmenides, Plato, and Aristotle, transcendent being was apprehended as *Nous*, a Greek term that can be translated as "Divine Intelligence." Human *nous* (intellect, mind) was experienced as a *participation* in transcendent divine *Nous*, and it is this divine *Nous*, they wrote, that orders reality and "steers all things through all things" (Heraclitus).[6] The consequences of this notion of transcendence for examining the world proved exceptional. For a world, a universe, formed by divine *Nous* is *intelligible structure itself*. And a universe that is essentially intelligible structure invites systematic explanatory investigation. The gateway to exploring the world scientifically had been found.

CHAPTER EIGHT

Science

The advent and progress of science in Western culture now needs to be considered, if briefly, since the world of modern scientific explanation and technological invention must be shown to be compatible with affirmations of inherent human dignity.[1] We can begin by asking what it is that science, as popularly understood, concerns itself with, meaning in this case the knowledge pursued in the natural sciences, and in the social sciences insofar as they investigate observable behavior. Answer: the natural world of sense-based empirical observation.

The issue of whether there can also be "empirical" study of data that is not sense-data—specifically, data of human consciousness—will concern us later. Scientific investigations in this sense are possible only because the natural world has been conceptually released, out of compact experiences of the cosmos, into relative autonomy. But scientific modes of examination are not the primary manner in which modern persons encounter nature in its relative autonomy. Much more basically, the universe of space and time is experienced as the place where we moderns live. "Lived experience" of the world precedes and contextualizes any specialized investigations of nature through scientific inquiry and insight.

35

Everyday lived experience is, indeed, the *sole* manner in which almost all of us experience—as modern adults—a world that has been de-divinized. It is our encompassing environment or "natural home" here on earth, domed by the day and night skies, where in our normal concerns and activities we interact with family members and friends, solve practical tasks, learn to use and appreciate tools, find beauty in nature and art, exercise ourselves in play and seek entertainment, deal with illness and sadness, and in general try to shape an existential story that feels like a satisfying performance in the human drama into which we have been born.

Making a living, getting around, cooking, building, organizing, adventuring, in an experientially postdifferentiated state of perception (not forgetting that our underlying experience of reality is still that of a cosmos, a completeness of meanings), all these activities occur in a "natural world" that is no longer inhabited by gods and goddesses, by numinous intracosmic forces, by immediate divine presences. The modern technician, nurse, farmer, businessman, politician, or musician inhabits a secular world, that is, a world where things can be understood, and actions engaged in, without at all needing to take into account their relationships with divine or ultimate meaning.

But then there is also—and this first appears with the ancient Greeks—that manner of coming to understand the meanings making up the immanent universe that is the scientific mode of engagement. What happens in this mode of inquiry, discovery, and expression is that a desire emerges to understand things more *systematically* than in terms of how they satisfy our needs and desires in practical ways, or how they appeal to us aesthetically, or however else they might be understood in their relations to us and our sensory perceptions. What happens is that the human desire to know asks, What is *invariable* about things? For example, what is fire in itself, always and anywhere? A corresponding ethical investigation was famously initiated by Socrates, What is courage in itself? Justice in itself, in any soul or society? This is the mode of questioning and coming to understand that the ancient Greeks called *theoria*. And from it has arisen what we generally call "science."

The distinguishing feature of scientific understanding is that it offers *systematic explanations* of things in terms of their intrinsic properties, in terms of their inherent developmental natures and tendencies (think biology and evolution), and, generally, in terms of the "relations constituted by the uniform interactions of things with one another" (Lonergan).[2] Notice that mention of divine intentions or divine presence is unnecessary (and alien) here, since these are explanations of intelligible structures *immanent* in the order of the universe, of the structures and forces in, of, and among natural things that make them appear and behave the way they do.

But the problematic thing for most of us about scientific accounts and their terminology—and there's no way around this—is that they are not just more (or better) insights of the same kind as our everyday, sense-based understandings. Explaining things in terms of "intrinsic properties" and "uniform interactions," which in physics and chemistry are based fundamentally in measurements, and in organic sciences in data pertaining to stages of development, involves new kinds of insights that open up new, abstract fields of knowledge. And these new kinds of insights require new technical languages corresponding to their peculiar kinds of intelligibilities, the intelligibilities of things understood, not in terms of their practical or aesthetic *relations to us*, but in terms of their *relations to one other*.[3] In relation to our senses, fire is bright and warm; in the terms of chemical science, fire is an exothermic reaction entailing oxidation, a language that doesn't describe, but explains.

Technical scientific languages inevitably baffle the nonscientist—have you ever listened to a conversation between physicists about their work?—even though scientific meanings pertain to the natural world we all experience. Their relevance and utility are also confirmed, of course, through experiments carried out in the world-as-observed, but they are comprehensible as scientific meanings only through understanding their essentially abstract languages of theoretical explanation. Sometimes, in our everyday nonscientific consciousness, we resent this fact.

The idea and practice of science historically develops. First came the (essentially Greek) conception of classical science, whose aim was to obtain absolutely certain and unimprovable knowledge of what is necessarily so. Modern scientific ideals and methods, however, transformed this idea of *theoria* into the more dynamic sciences with which we are familiar today (if only in popular appreciation of them). In the modern sciences, what is to be explained includes not only the dependably causal laws of relations between things, but also the concrete particularities of natural events. And so beyond classical laws that apply in all known cases of certain relations between things (for example, the mathematical regularity of the law of falling bodies formulated by Galileo), science discovers ways of explaining, in terms of statistical laws of occurrence, the *random* aspect of events and their convergences, for example, the statistical prediction that in a certain locality there is a 45 percent chance of precipitation tomorrow. And, in the organic sciences, ways of explaining, for example, growth and adaptation both in individuals and in species, the emergence of organizationally higher life-forms (plant, animal, human), and how distinct kinds of living things interact with their environments.

For modern science, therefore relevant data includes—in addition to data susceptible to explanation by abstract laws explaining unvarying regularities—all the *variations* that one can find in the universe, all the *differences* things and events can display, all the interrelated *schemes of probability* flowing from specified initial conditions, even abnormalities, and the breakdowns of typical or normative development. The guiding ideal in modern science is a never-ending (and never-realizable) search to determine the intelligible relations that explain *all* the objects and events in the universe. It is a search understood now to be a process yielding not (as Aristotle had hoped) a perfect grasp of what must exist (and indeed nothing in the spatiotemporal universe exists of necessity), but only better and better approximations of explanatory truth in the form of verified hypotheses always open to revision.

What is consistent from the ancient through the modern sciences, though, is that objects are to be explained as they are "in themselves," that is, in terms of their intrinsic properties and of things in their relations to each other. Modern science, however, dramatically changed the game: first, by applying measurement as the basic intelligibility of physical relationships; second, by intending theoretical explanations of all worldly data; third, by recognizing and accounting for evolution and adaptation, and variabilities of actual and probable emergence; and, fourth, by grounding its verifications in experiments. In this way knowledge in each scientific field and subfield has come to be viewed as an ongoing process of discovery and revision for which methods for advance and application continue to be worked out.

Science 39

Both the explanatory vistas opened up by the modern sciences and the technologies they have made possible—the tools in our daily lives, which fascinate (and overwhelm) us—have led some to view the scientific mode of knowing as the only kind that reveals what is true and real about the world. But this outlook has inevitably engendered a backlash: many voices in our culture insist on the importance of recognizing the complementarity of scientific truths, on the one hand, and those of everyday common sense (and of scholarship, and art, and philosophy, and religion, and spirituality), on the other. Which is scarcely surprising, given the following facts.

First, for the vast majority of persons, for whom the technical languages of the sciences are closed books, meanings are grasped solely through the kinds of understanding that belong to everyday (i.e., nonscientific) modes of experience. Thus, for the vast majority of people, all thoughts about the meaningfulness of their lives are grounded in nonscientific insights.

Second, the realm of *nature* includes, rather problematically, *human nature*. But full and proper explanations of human nature must take into account not only the relevant data of sense (everything physically observable about human entities and their activities, from the neuroscience of brains to the behaviors of crowds), but also *the data of human consciousness*. The data of human consciousness is precisely spiritual data (i.e., not material data), and, technically, what makes human beings human and not merely a species of animal is "spirit" (Gr. *pneuma*; Heb. *ruach*). Human nature refers to a genus of being that participates in the cosmos as both body and spirit. That is, acts of distinctively human consciousness, such as those of self-aware understanding, knowing, and deciding—operations of mind—are in themselves nonphysical, though ontologically founded in and conditioned by bodily and animalic processes.

In Plato's *Phaedo*, Socrates expresses a charming exasperation with those unable to grasp this seemingly simple philosophical distinction between the operations of someone's mind and the physical conditions allowing that mind to guide and perform bodily actions in the world. When a person accepts "human being" for what it is, and also acknowledges that humans exist not solely in the universe conditioned by space and time but in a cosmos, then the spatio-temporal intelligibilities explained by the sciences receive their proper contextualization. The questions of science (understood as the natural and behavioral sciences) cannot, by definition, be concerned with the ground of the cosmos, which human consciousness, being spirit, spontaneously asks about, as any normal person does.

Third, ignoring the transcendent realm of meaning that grounds the immanent universe does not demolish it; it merely eclipses it. And what Freud calls the "return of the repressed" will have its day and its say.

Fourth, inherent human dignity is not a scientifically observable fact. If it exists, it does so as an invisible datum of worth (Ger., *Würde*, "dignity") whose truth is affirmable only insofar as it is recognized as *participation in the transcendent value of the ground of reality*.

Such an affirmation is both intelligent and intelligible. The intelligent and intelligible explanations of science, for their part, are concerned with the observable physical, chemical, biological, and animal-perceptual processes that found and condition, and so make possible in the world, the spiritual presence of human beings in their inherent dignity.

CHAPTER NINE

Misunderstanding Human Nature

When we ask what human nature is, the words themselves can be a cause of misdirection, since the word "nature" suggests that a complete answer to the question might be provided through a rigorous enough understanding of human immersion in "the natural world." But this is not the case, because in human consciousness, both immanent ("natural") and transcendent realms of meaning consciously meet and interpenetrate.

As a microcosmos, a human being shares in all of the strata of the hierarchy of being that appear as phenomena in the dynamically emergent universe. *Physical* schemes provide the foundations and conditions of *chemical* laws that are organized by *metabolic processes*, which ground bodily health and activity and in turn underlie and make possible our *animal capacities* of perception, memory, and affect. Each of these levels of being can be scientifically examined in its function as constitutive of human existence. The social sciences study observable patterns of human behavior, and depth psychology and phenomenologies of perception, language, and inquiry yield accounts of the operations of human consciousness itself, operations made possible by the successful functioning of all the founding and conditioning underlying strata.

But even the scope of all such fields together does not exhaust those intelligibilities that constitute human nature, because each person, like the cosmos it reflects, is constituted also by that which transcends the world of space and time. Every human being is a *person*, and every person (each "face," Levinas says) reveals the presence of a "beyond" that is irreducible to intrinsically material processes.[1] The Greek philosophers who discovered the transcendent ground to be *Nous* (Intellect)—thereby opening to scientific analysis a universe understood as intrinsically intelligible in structure—emphasized that human psyches could make such a discovery only because a part, or aspect, of each human psyche is itself *nous*, and that this human *nous* is a participation in divine *Nous*. They also investigated what a human existence truly attuned to divine *Nous*, a "noetically well-ordered" existence, would look like. For them, as for adherents of each of the major Western and Eastern religious traditions, a proper exposition of human nature acknowledges that in humans both worldly structures and a self-presence of the transcendent ground of order that ordains and sustains worldly structures are mixed in some sort of unity.

The question that all of these traditions bequeathed to ensuing generations is, How are we to understand this unique mixture of immanent being and conscious participation in transcendence, which every human being is? In Western cultures, within the vast array of attempts to take up and respond to this question, one can distinguish two basic modes of inquiry and expression. One of these entails increasingly nuanced *descriptions* (portrayals) of humans as self-aware participants in both worldly and transcendent reality. One can trace this stream of exploration from Plato and the writers of the Hebrew scriptures through such eminent figures as Augustine, Dante, Goethe, Shakespeare, and Dostoyevsky, on up to literary modernists, including T. S. Eliot and Marcel Proust.

Complementarily, there is a stream of abstract, philosophically *explanatory* accounts of human being as a "site" co-constituted by worldly structures and conscious participation in transcendent reality, which formally begins with Aristotle's "science of the human" and continues through subsequent classical and medieval expansions and revisions (including those of Arabic philosophy). In this initial scientific mode, such explanations aimed at establishing knowledge of what is necessary and unvarying about humans, abstracting from circumstantial contingencies, developmental particularities, and other variables that make individuals what they concretely are. Eventually, though, the modern "turn to the subject"—associated with philosophers such as Descartes, Kant, Hegel, Husserl, and Lonergan—together with insights into the human as a distinct genus within evolutionary emergence with a unique range of capabilities, brought forth systematic, explanatory accounts that seek to take into consideration not only what is unvaryingly true and formally definitive about all human beings everywhere but also the particularity and historicity of human beings in distinct and varying cultures and as concrete individual subjects, each of whom has a unique personal story and—once mature enough—carries the responsibility of self-management.

Whatever oversights may be attributed to the authors of either descriptive or explanatory analyses of human existence that present it as a unified mixture of immanent being and participation in transcendent presence, none of them commits the elementary philosophical blunder of presuming that human existence is a merely worldly mode of being. Many influential philosophers, and other influential thinkers and writers and teachers, *have* made this blunder, just as have many people of supposed common sense, from the cultural time of the classical Greeks to that of the present day. It is a blunder that has infected modern thinking in a peculiarly virulent way, in part because of the influence on popular imagination of the successes of the natural sciences in explaining the spatiotemporal world and the attendant showering upon us of the amazing tools that these successes have made possible. Scientific and technological involvement with all that is worldly has contributed to making hugely alluring and popular "immanentist," or reductively worldly, interpretations of human nature, in which transcendent reality is dismissed as an illusion. This despite the impressive logical non sequitur involved in that dismissal: for since science and technology, pertaining as they do to the intelligible structures that constitute the spatiotemporal universe, have nothing to do with, and cannot reasonably ask about, a transcendent reality, they obviously can neither prove nor disprove it.

Already in the eighteenth century, Enlightenment enthusiasm at the prospect of the natural sciences producing a complete causal explanation of human nature and behavior led to such visions as presented in Julien Offray de La Mettrie's *Man a Machine* (*L'homme machine*) (1748). More recently, in the same immanentist vein, the evolutionary biologist E. O. Wilson has written that a proper worldview would be based on the assumption that "all tangible phenomena, from the birth of the stars to the workings of *social* institutions are materially based and ultimately reducible . . . to the laws of physics" (italics mine).[2]

Probably the most popular contemporary scientistic-immanentist trend in thinking about people is to envision humans as merely supremely sophisticated computers. Conversely, part of the current fascination with so-called artificial intelligence (AI), exhibits the perennial sci-fi imagining of computers becoming conscious—both aware and aware of themselves as aware—and therefore ontologically indistinguishable from humans.

Immanentist conceptions of human nature come in other modes, however, than imaginative reductions of humans to material processes (still the basis of AI—or, better named, Artificial Computation, Retrieval, and Integrative Display) that would, in principle, be fully explainable by one or another of the natural sciences, whether interpretation's crown be accorded to physics, chemistry, neuroscience, evolutionary biology, or some other immanentist explanatory account of human-as-emergent. There are also, for example, *sociological* immanentisms, where the entire meaning of existence is interpreted as the product of social forces and influences, and the value of individuals is identified with how much they contribute (or might contribute) to the survival and functioning of a society. This is the kind of sociological reduction that was presented by Bolshevik ideology, where the value and purposes of persons were judged in terms of their contributions to the creation of "communist society."

The blunder of immanentism doesn't have to take such severe forms as physicalism, or evolutionary biologism, or—what should it be called?—reductive sociologicalism. For it is possible to appreciate the psychological complexities of individuals *as* individuals, to affirm each to be a center of value, to recognize humans as having essential freedom, to acknowledge the "interiority" of human cognitional process as an autonomous level of being, and *still* to conceive of human nature, along with reality as a whole, as only "worldly," that is, as consisting only of spatiotemporal identities, characteristics, processes, and events. Human beings can still be viewed, even granted the realities of human intelligence and free deliberation, as worldly things among other worldly things, in a universe that is imagined to be an all-encompassing thing that contains all the things inside it.

This is an incoherent view, in that both freedom and the conscious operations entailed in pursuing and satisfying the human desire to know are not things in the manner of physical entities, but rather manifestations of spiritual (i.e., nonphysical) reality. But combining the influence of human thinking's default assumption that reality is composed only of data accessible to sense-perception and observation, and the effect of the eclipse of transcendent reality, modern appreciators of human interior complexity, depth, and strangeness simply have no alternative but to regard humans as immanent things within a solely immanent reality.

The basic problem with all immanentist accounts is that their explanations of human nature ignore the fact that human existence is participation in a cosmos, and that the notion of immanence as the whole of reality is the product of a philosophical oversight. The cosmos can indeed be differentiated into immanent and transcendent dimensions (a differentiating discovery, we need to be reminded, that occurs only within consciousnesses), but it still remains the one cosmos composed of the world plus its mysterious ground. Immanentism ignores the mysterious ground, and thus ignores the cosmos.

If one is faithful to remembrance of the cosmos, there are only two satisfying answers to the question about the ground of human existence and the world. Either the ground of reality is in essence the enduring gods and goddesses and their numinous cohorts as expressed in countless cosmological myths, and revived in contemporary neopaganism, neopolytheism, and embraces of occultism and magic; or, the ground is essentially a transcendent reality, as identified in spiritual breakthroughs, such as the discovery of the Tao, of the Hindu *Brahman* and the transcendent affirmed in Buddhist teachings, of the Greek *Nous*, of the God of Judaism, of the Triune God of Christianity, of the Allah of Islam. In each of these spiritual breakthroughs, human consciousness—and thus human nature—finds itself to be co-constituted by conscious participation in transcendent reality.

Therefore, within the horizon of human self-understanding established by these cosmos-differentiating traditions (traditions that established, whether we like it or not, the conceptual and linguistic horizons of the modern inheritance), honesty entails acknowledging, respectfully and responsibly, that human nature transcends the arena of spatiotemporal nature that modern science continues to explain and exploit.

CHAPTER TEN

Constants of Human Nature

The essence of human nature is participation in both nature and what transcends nature. Humans are those beings in whom consciousness is capable of apprehending—and ontologically shows—the distinction and relationship between the world and a world-transcending ground of being. A human being is human, in other words, in part because of *openness to* transcendent reality, *participation in* transcendent reality, and the *showing-forth of* transcendent reality. In Western religious terms, this has been expressed by saying that human beings are where God and world consciously encounter each other, with persons having, consequently, the responsibility to remain in openness to the divine ground of order (and to writings and teachings deriving from this openness), and the obligation to act in a manner reflecting the influence of such openness.

Consider all the contributions to anthropological understanding by studies of cultural, political, linguistic, psychological, biological, chemical, and evolutionary processes, all of them structures intrinsic to being human. In light of these studies, to ask, What is human nature? is to evoke vast torrents of explanation, ranging from this year's accounts of brain neuroscience to analyses of the most esoteric mysticisms. And yet all of these discoveries and investigations (presuming their soundness) go toward complementing, and never annul, the historically foundational philosophical insight that human nature is the peculiar "in-between" mode of participating in the process of reality where immanent and transcendent realms of meaning consciously intersect.

We can draw from this foundational philosophical insight a cluster of elemental facts about human nature, remembering that an account of something's nature entails identifying constants that belong to it, constants manifested under all historical circumstances and in every individual case. The following is a delineation of *constants of human nature* that answers to the known facts of human history and to the history of the differentiations of transcendence East and West. It will also serve as a kind of summary of reflections in my nine previous chapters.

First, there is a *unique manner in which human beings participate in reality*. A human is a (relatively) autonomous being that consciously knows that it exists, consciously wonders about its existence, and consciously seeks to understand the intelligibilities that make up reality. This human seeking of understanding, the individual's desire to know, is simultaneously a being-drawn-toward-knowing by the mysterious ground of reality that is present in each consciousness as a restless "notion of being."[1] Because human consciousness is in its essence a seeking that is also a being-drawn, it may be described, Voegelin explains, as a *tension*, and because this tension is a participation in the cosmos, it may be called a *participatory tension*.[2] This is one constant regarding human nature.

Second, there is a human *awareness of the cosmos* to which we belong. As the human search for meaning has advanced in its historically differentiating course, the understood structures within the order of reality have expanded enormously, but the cosmos, for all that, does not and cannot disintegrate as a grounding fact in the human comprehension of reality. The cosmos remains present to human consciousness as the Whole within which all meanings are understood and all knowledge occurs, as the anticipated narrative completeness of meaning within which all concern, questioning, knowing, and loving take place.

Third is that the participatory tension of consciousness that each person is includes *awareness of and a desire to know the ground of being*. Human consciousness is always aware that it is not the cause of its own existence; therefore, at the center of consciousness there is a desire to grasp what its own ground truly is. Because of this, every human being is constituted, by nature, as a *tension toward the ground* (Voegelin), a desiring concern to understand the ultimate basis of the cosmos, and thereby the whys and wherefores of its own existence.[3]

Fourth is that *the object of the human search for understanding is meaning*. We want to understand the meanings that make up the intelligible structures of reality, we desire to know the meaning of the ground of being, and we want to grasp those meanings that will guide us toward personal and communal fulfillment. Historically, consciousness unfolds as a long search for the meanings of things, causes, values, and the ground of being, developing from cosmologically compact forms of knowing into the differentiated appreciations of social, political, technological, artistic, and cultural life with which we are familiar.

Fifth, the *process of seeking meaning*—the inquiry-and-feeling-driven thinking process—also has its internal constants: the recurrent pattern of intelligibly related operations that make up the functioning of the human "mind."

These have been clarified especially well by Bernard Lonergan, as follows.[4] To begin with, we question: a human being *is* the Question.[5] But questioning is never about nothing; it is always about something— something experiential—it is an effort to discover meanings in data made present to us through experiences. The most obvious experiential data are those encountered through the five outward-directed senses and the data of inner sensations and emotions. At some point in our development, we become aware of our experiences of self-awareness, of our thinking activities, of our decision-making. We recognize that the data encountered here are not data of sense, but *data of consciousness*, consisting of many nonsensorily observable operations, all propelled by desire, shot through with emotions, and accompanied by self-awareness.

Whether the data of experience focused on by questioning are data of sense or data of consciousness, what questioning initially aims for is an *understanding* of data—more precisely, an understanding of intelligible structures (forms) that might be present in the data. Any such act of understanding (experienced as an illumination of meaning) Lonergan names an "insight," and through such insights, intelligence ontologically becomes the intelligibility understood ("intelligence in act" and "intelligibility in act" are one and the same).

When we arrive at an insight into experienced data (which is not inevitable; our questioning may be frustrated), our inquiring nature moves on to a new target. For a further question arises, Is my insight correct? Early in life we come to realize that insights may be mistaken. Awareness of this leads us (normatively, anyway) to consider, after having had an insight, if there is *sufficient evidence* to assure us that our insight is in fact correct, that it corresponds to the way things are in reality. When we are confident that we have discovered sufficient evidence supporting our insight, the norms inherent in our inquiring nature compel us—if we are being rational—to make a *judgment of fact* in which we claim (internally and perhaps to others) that our insight is true, or, if there is sufficient contradictory evidence, to make a judgment that it is *not* true, or, to make a judgment that the truth of our insight is merely probable, or possible, or unlikely, and so forth.

It is a person's cumulative judgments of fact that constitute a (presumptive) horizon of knowledge. "Presumptive" because we know that we sometimes make errors of judgment. There are two further basic recurrent operations to be noted in the human thinking process.

First, on the basis of the knowledge (real and presumed) that a person regards as pertinent to a given situation, we make a *decision* about how to act. Most of our decisions are minor and of little consequence: what to eat for breakfast, whether or not to take a walk. Some are self-determinative. A few are existentially momentous. How do we arrive at decisions? In a given situation, we realize that we have a range of options regarding actions we might take in a given situation, and we *deliberate* about these, drawing both on our knowledge and on the feelings attracting us toward this or that preferred action. Which feelings? Perhaps we will let ourselves decide in favor of the most pleasurable (or least painful) option. Perhaps, alternatively, we find feelings in ourselves that arise from awareness that a certain act appears to be the most *worthwhile* among our options, that which is of the greatest value, and we let this feeling draw us into moral considerations culminating in a corresponding *judgment of value* ("This action will be best"), which becomes the basis for a decision, and for action. Judgments of value can, of course, be erroneous, just like judgments of fact. Growth in virtue, like growth in learning, involves continual self-correction.

And finally, questioning, understanding, searching for evidence, attaining knowledge through judgments of fact, evaluating courses of action, and deciding, all reach fruition in *acts of loving*. To love is to *will the good of a being* (a being that may be oneself). It is in acts of loving that the native drive of human inquiry—the unrestricted desire to understand and to "become all things," to know other persons and objects within the Whole of what is, and to bring values, or goods, into being that wouldn't exist if we didn't decide for them—finds its fulfillment, its proper term. For now, let us merely note that when I am loving, it is self-evident to me that this is what my conscious questioning, experiencing, knowing, and choosing have ultimately been for.

Thus, in sum, one may identify as a fifth constant in human nature *a dynamism of related and recurrent cognitional operations*, operations that may be identified as the questioning of experiences, understanding through insight, judging, deliberating and deciding, and loving. This structure of recurrent dynamic operations—which is how thinking works—constitutes a fifth constant to supplement the first four constants.

How might one verify all of these constants, including the details in this account of how we think? Verifications that would grant us some trustworthy existential orientation in response to the elemental questions, Where am I? What is this reality called the world? What am I? By attending (honestly and courteously) to experiences revealing of oneself and one's situation in reality, by inquiring diligently, and by finding sufficient evidence to ground them as true judgments of fact.

PART 2

The Idea of Inherent Human Dignity

CHAPTER ELEVEN

Inherent Human Dignity

The idea of inherent human dignity has come to play a prominent role in modern culture, in part because it is central to modern theories of human rights, in which it serves as an anchor to stabilize arguments as to why human beings have rights to begin with. The modern argument linking inherent dignity and rights is this: because, it is claimed, human beings have an inherent value (dignity), they also possess various rights whose purpose is the protection of human existence and the promotion of its distinctive type of flourishing. But the concept of inherent human dignity brings with it a host of philosophical difficulties. To begin with there are disagreements about how exactly to define it. It asserts a value that belongs to being human, but how are we to understand the content or substance of this value? Then there are questions about how it should function when used, as increasingly it is, as a factor in legal decisions, and in jurisprudence generally. More recently, the idea has been criticized as expressing an anthropocentric disregard of the intrinsic value of animals (and indeed of plants). And then there are not a few who simply deny the validity of the concept, dismissing it as a product of metaphysical sentimentalism, or a relic of outmoded religious belief.

Despite these criticisms, the idea has become ever-more ubiquitous in modern journalistic, political, and legal discourse. And that has created a pressure to explicate the concept, to clarify its substantive meaning and to spell out its philosophical implications. I propose the following brief description of the substantive meaning of the concept.

The idea of inherent human dignity is that of a value belonging uniquely to humans and intrinsic to them because of distinctive qualities that belong to human nature. These qualities include (1) the capacities of self-aware questioning, understanding, and knowing (that is, the seeking and grasping of intelligibilities through insights and the ability to verify the truth of those insights); (2) the capacity to apprehend that which is morally valuable, to freely affirm values already in existence, to recognize moral courses of action, and to perform good actions; (3) the capacity for self-transcending love; (4) the capacity for creativity that arises from the combination of imagination, insight, freedom, and moral deliberation and decision; (5) the self-determination that all these capacities in combination make possible; (6) the radical uniqueness, and irreplaceability, of this self; and (7) the fragility that belongs to each of these capacities singly and together, as humans beings remain always vulnerable to disruptions of their proper functions, and also to physical and emotional suffering.

This is not meant to be a final and definitive definition of the idea. But this formulation gets at the essence, I believe, of what writings about inherent human dignity refer to. The words and phrases I've used here are not what is key. Important are the insights that underlie the words and phrases used to articulate these seven components that together inform the idea of inherent human dignity. The insights might have been expressed here in somewhat different words and phrases, but these insights, not the words I've used, carry the weight of my discussions here and below.

Some of the philosophical implications of the idea of inherent human dignity are as follows. First, an inherent dignity, or value, is one that is present whether or not it is recognized by other persons (or goes unrecognized even by the person to whom it belongs). It is not the fruit of any kind of social agreement or contract; it does not arise out of any pragmatic considerations or arrangements. It is not a human construction. If this inherent value exists, it does so regardless of what anyone might think about the matter (and even if no thought at all is given to it), and the most forceful denunciations of its truth, or the ignoring of its existence, have no effect upon it. Such an inherent dignity is a *given*, and remains so under all conditions, whether it has been overlooked, as often in the past, or it is increasingly honored as a political principle.

Second, if it is true that each human being has an inherent dignity (and consequently inherent rights that would, if legally observed, protect and promote human existence and flourishing), then neither the differences between human beings and situations nor the transience of human circumstances affects that truth. If inherent dignity is a given that belongs to human nature, then every instance of that dignity is a fact that transcends all differences in biology, locality, culture, and history.

If differences among human beings and situations do not affect the intrinsic value of humans, then the reality of that value belongs to an unalterable ground of meaning in which human existence participates, rather than to the changing worldly conditions that go toward constituting that existence. Only the grounding, the participation, of human value in a transcendent realm of meaning would give a truth of inherent human dignity the status of an absolute, a truth that admits of no exceptions, a truth beyond human power to undermine, a truth "beyond the possibility of any revocation by merely human means," says Gerhard Sauter.[1]

In order to honor the process of the philosophical discovery of this idea, we must pause to note the historical relationship between the notion of *inherent human dignity* and the notion of *transcendent reality*. The foregoing reflections began by considering the concept of inherent human dignity, an idea central to modern conceptions of human rights and (at least tacitly) of human nature, and proceeded to deduce that, to be unalterably and absolutely true, inherent human value must be grounded in a realm of transcendent meaning. But in terms of the history of human thought, such a deduction puts the cart before the horse.

For the idea of inherent human dignity is not one clue, among others, that might lead philosophical reflection to conclude that there is a transcendent realm of meaning. Rather the idea itself is a consequence of differentiated experiences of the presence of transcendent reality in human consciousness, experiences on the part of those seekers into the truth of the ground of the cosmos who have differentiated it into transcendent and immanent realms of meaning. Historically, that is, the human discoveries that the ground of reality is a transcendent realm of meaning, and that it is possible to recognize this because human consciousness shares an identity with this transcendence—for example, human *nous* is a *participation* in divine *Nous*; human *pneuma* is a *participation* in the divine Spirit—have led to the emergence, over time, to the recognition that every human being shares in and shows forth the transcendent ground of reality.

With this clarified, we can note that a third philosophical implication of the idea of inherent human dignity is that affirming it to be true is to affirm that each person has a value deriving from personal participation in the imperishable and perfect value of transcendent reality. It is for this reason, Immanuel Kant famously explained, that the inherent dignity of each person should be regarded as an unconditioned and incomparable worth that deserves our "reverence."[2]

Fourth, in many modern political documents regarding human rights and international law (or legal ideals), it is emphasized that all human beings share *equally* in the inherent dignity (infinite value) that belongs to persons by nature. Since the worth of human dignity is infinite, and each person shares in this infinite worth, how could it be otherwise?

But here a global historical question appears. The discovery of the participation of human consciousness in a transcendent realm of meaning first occurred in advanced cultures both East and West in the first millennium BCE. One such culture was that of Hindu religious philosophy, where the Upanishads (ca. 800–200 BCE) taught that the most intimate, deepest Self of each person (*atman*) is an identity with the impersonal transcendent ground of all reality, *Brahman*. Transcendent value is thus *present* in every person. And yet, no doctrine of equal inherent human dignity (inherent equal human value) appeared in Hindu thought and teaching (note the emphasis in the Upanishads on the Brahmin class, and also their portrayals of the status of women.) Why not?

Let us answer by noting an ambiguity in the word "presence." The Upanishads teach that if one is sufficiently meditatively disciplined, one may discover that *Brahman* is "present" as one's deepest

Self. But this being present of transcendent reality in each person is not ultimately a presence such as that referred to when we say we are in the presence of a friend. The latter is the presence of personhood. *Brahman* is said to be recognized, in perfected insight, not as the manifestation of a god (such as Vishnu, Brahma, or Shiva) but, rather, as an impersonal transcendent principle. But the presence of a person, to use Martin Buber's language, is the presence of a You (or Thou).

We must imagine individuals who experienced the basic differentiation of the cosmos into natural world and transcendence discovering the "presence of transcendence" to be, not the presence of an impersonal principle, but that of a divine You. In this case, the innate value (dignity) inherent in each human being would be that of the one infinite divine You.[3] Each human would be a shared presence of God, and each person would equally be deserving of reverence, since — however spiritually aware or spiritually developed or spiritually responsible one might be — each person would equally be an instance of this divine presence embodied.

Precisely this is what is understood to have occurred in Jewish and Christian differentiations of the cosmos into immanent world and transcendent divine being. Judaism and Christianity have famously declared that each person is made "in the image and likeness of God," an assertion subject to and productive of seemingly endless theological interpretations over centuries, but basically asserting that human persons are partakers in, and transparencies for, the infinite value of transcendent divine personhood. But the word "person" itself — the Latin *persona* — was not applied to the God of radical transcendence until the advent of Trinitarian Christianity, where the three "persons" of the Trinity were affirmed amidst clarification that personhood is *of its essence* a relation among persons.

This is why the historical emergence of the notion of the absolute equal value of all persons was culture-specific. It was foreign to all ancient and cosmological cultures. It did not arise in the wake of the Chinese discovery of the Tao, or in the wake of the Hindu discovery of the transcendent principle of *Brahman*, and it is not to be found in Confucianism. Buddhism teaches the ability of all to *become* enlightened, but not of an already-existing *fact* of equal personhood.

The historical reality is that notions of inherent human dignity and of inalienable human rights emerged and developed out of

Hebrew, Jewish, and Christian "encounters with God." And over time, in agonies of conceiving—and through the gradual overturning of established traditions, practices, habits, viewpoints, and biases of all kinds—it was brought to bear, initially only in the West, on legal, political, and cultural views and institutions. Ever so gradually and fitfully.

CHAPTER TWELVE

Inherent Dignity in the Universal Declaration of Human Rights (I)

The United Nations was founded in October 1945. Eight months later, it established its Commission on Human Rights, which was given the task of producing an international "bill of rights." The resulting document—the outcome of two years of discussion, drafting, revision, and gradual agreement on the part of UN members representing eighteen nations with often sharply divergent political traditions and viewpoints—was the Universal Declaration of Human Rights (UDHR), ratified on December 10, 1948.

Despite their political differences, what above all kept commission members devoted to their common purpose was knowledge of the barbarisms and massacres committed during World War II and shock over the discovery of Nazi death camps—systematized atrocities constructed on the premise that some races, some ethnic groups, some nationalities, some persons of this or that condition or persuasion either were of negligibly significant human status or were not genuinely human at all, but rather subhuman and harmful entities, all of whom should be exterminated. More than any other factor, the extermination camps brought the commission's members into solidarity in the conviction that, as representatives of the world community, they were morally required to articulate and promulgate a universal code of human rights as an expression of world conscience in response to such atrocities.

It was clear from the outset, however, that given the diverse political visions and principles represented within the commission's membership, its international bill of rights would have to employ a language that was pragmatic rather than theoretical, that is, a language that avoided all metaphysical and religious formulations. Common agreement on the ontological (metaphysical) basis of human rights was out of the question.

This explains the purely secular character of the UDHR. Even an unprovocative reference in Article 1 to "nature" as the source of human reason and conscience, present through most of the drafts, was finally deleted primarily because it was deemed by objectors to carry a hint of the Enlightenment idea of Nature as the creation of God. The document ultimately ratified was one that, according to René Cassin (French delegate and one of the four key drafters), "allowed the Committee to take no position on the nature of man and of society and to avoid metaphysical controversies, notably the conflicting doctrines of spiritualists, rationalists, and materialists regarding the origin of the rights of man."[1]

Still, the drafters of the document had to give some indication as to *why it is* that human beings have what is identified in the UDHR as "inalienable rights," including rights to life, liberty, security, to ownership of property, to equal recognition and obligation under law, to legal protection against discrimination, and to freedoms of expression, religious worship, association, and other freedoms. What is the basis for asserting that human beings have such rights?

The preclusion of any religious or metaphysical answer meant that the drafters could not have recourse to the idea, proclaimed by the U.S. Declaration of Independence, that persons are endowed by a Creator with certain "unalienable rights." Nor could they allow such rights to derive from the state, or any other social organ, since something socially conferred can, on principle, be socially rescinded. The drafters solved this problem by indicating that human beings have rights because of their *inherent dignity*, because human beings, out of the qualities they possess (i.e., human nature), have a special value, a distinctive worth, that in each case and without exception should be respected and nourished. Thus, the UDHR's first words proclaim the "inherent dignity" of each member of the human family.

This relationship of dependence—of rights deriving from dignity—is not, it is true, what the opening clause of the UDHR's preamble states. It simply affirms, first, a fact of "inherent dignity," and then a fact of "inalienable rights," and does not state that the latter derive from the former: "Whereas recognition of the inherent dignity and of the equal and inalienable rights of all members of the human family is the foundation of freedom, justice and peace in the world . . ."

One might reasonably question, then, the claim that the document was intended to present human dignity as the basis of human rights. But it turns out that this claim is supported by considerable evidence. Records available to anyone wishing to examine the history of the composition of the UDHR reveal that three of the four commission members most influential in its ultimate shaping—the Lebanese delegate Charles Malik, the U.S. delegate Eleanor Roosevelt, and the Chinese delegate P. C. Chang—understood the relationship between dignity and rights precisely in this way. The fourth key shaper was the French delegate, Cassin.

I present a few pieces of evidence. First, at the first official meeting of the Commission on Human Rights in January 1947, Chang suggested—amid general agreement—that the UDHR should include a preamble that set forth the premise on which the document's assertion of rights was based, and that the concept of human dignity should be elevated to serve just that purpose. Then, in June 1948, when the South African delegate C. T. Te Water suggested removing the term "dignity" from the document altogether (a telling signal of apartheid-based politics), Eleanor Roosevelt responded, reports Mary Ann Glendon, by explaining that in the scheme of the UDHR, Article 1—which affirms universal, equal, and inherent human dignity— "did not refer to [any] specific rights because it was meant to explain *why human beings have rights to begin with.*"[2] Finally, in June 1948, when Malik—a philosopher by training and an academic, but also a diplomat and politician—composed the final version of the preamble, he made sure that the very first words of the document affirmed inherent dignity with the explicit intention, he said, of indicating why human beings have rights.

There are a number of later UN documents that make explicit this relationship of the derivation of rights from inherent dignity. Perhaps most notable are the two complementary covenants, the International Covenant on Civil and Political Rights (1965) and the International Covenant on Economic, Social and Cultural Rights (1966), and the Convention against Torture and Other Cruel, Inhuman or Degrading Treatment or Punishment (1984). All three documents begin with the assertion that human rights "derive from the inherent dignity of the human person."

The Helsinki Final Act of 1975 reaffirms this derivation of rights from inherent dignity, as does the Vienna Declaration adopted by the World Conference on Human Rights in 1993. Inherent human dignity is thus, beyond question, intended to be understood as the founding fact upon which rests the affirmation of human rights in the UDHR.

Why is this clarification so important? Because of the enormity of the influence of the UDHR. Its affirmations of human dignity and rights, and its principal authors' understanding of inherent dignity as the basis of inalienable rights, have been echoed in many charters, conventions, and constitutions produced around the world since 1948. For example, in the Basic Law for the Federal Republic of Germany (1949), the famous first words of which are "Human dignity shall be inviolable. To respect and protect it shall be the duty of all state authority," and in the postapartheid Constitution of the Republic of South Africa (1996), which pronounces the nation to be founded on "unalterable" values, the first of which is "human dignity."

The extraordinary influence of the UDHR through (and radiating beyond) political documents is, in fact, one reason why references to human dignity have become so ubiquitous not only among politicians and legalists, but in journalism and in general conversation. The ratification and promulgation of the UDHR turns out to have been a kind of "moment zero" in which the concept of inherent human dignity began to be propelled to the center of everyday political and cultural discourse, but it had long been a staple of theological, and modern philosophical and political, writings.

One might wonder, though, how often everyday moralists who nowadays speak of human dignity (referring to *inherent* dignity) have a clear grasp of the meaning of the idea, not to mention its philosophical implications. Freighted language symbols such as *inherent dignity*, after all, arise from and are meant to convey specific insights, insights in which specific intelligibilities have been grasped in the course of striving to understand the data present in certain experiences. With regard to inherent human dignity, we can ask, Which intelligibilities? What experiences? Which data? The principal drafters of the UDHR had cogent and intriguing answers to those questions, even if they could not, for political reasons, mention them in the document.

CHAPTER THIRTEEN

Inherent Dignity in the Universal Declaration of Human Rights (II)

The four members of the UN Commission on Human Rights responsible for crafting the final version of the Universal Declaration of Human Rights (UDHR)—Charles Malik, Eleanor Roosevelt, P. C. Chang, and René Cassin—knew that the document's concept of equal inherent human dignity carried specific historical baggage. To shorten a long story: the word "dignity" derives from the Latin *dignitas*, which in Roman culture referred to the social influence and prestige belonging to a man of respected rank and moral repute (and to the respect due to his family). But the term gradually became associated less with social status and honor and more with indwelling human value—specifically, with the idea of the nobility of human reason emphasized by Stoic philosophers, and with Jewish and Christian ideas of human being as *imago Dei*—as made "in the image and likeness of God."

Western expositions on human dignity up to and beyond the Enlightenment were built, mainly, on the scaffolding of Christian anthropology, which elaborated the *imago Dei* symbol. A human being was viewed as a creature who, in a limited way, participates in the powers of reasoning, moral concern, freedom, love, and creativity that belong (perfectly) to divine transcendent being. Patristic and medieval writings on human dignity, early modern political texts on natural law and natural rights, Renaissance humanist ideas, Enlightenment declarations about "the rights of man," and Kant's influential account of dignity—all reflect this vision of the individual as *imago Dei*. They also emphasize that each person (1) is unique and irreplaceable, and (2) shares an obligation to respect the divine presence in other persons.

Political arguments for liberal democracy as the most appropriate, if fragile, human political arrangement are also historically rooted in this Christianly elaborated vision of human existence, since liberal democracy politically institutionalizes a vision of each person as inherently of incalculable worth, capable of the considered use of reason, and educable for a responsible exercise of freedom through conscience, awareness of duty, and love. The Christian anthropological vision of equal inherent human dignity is politically mirrored in self-determining democratic polities made functionally effective through governments "of, by, and for the people," which protect against abuse of executive authority by effective separation of executive, legislative, and judicial powers, and which recognize all persons as equal before laws that protect the liberties (individual and associational) necessary for human flourishing.

Most of the members of the whole Commission on Human Rights responsible for drafting the UDHR were unconcerned with Christian anthropology or Christian belief in a transcendent source of human dignity. It was otherwise with the four key drafters. Malik was a member of the Greek Orthodox Church, and an ardent Thomist; Roosevelt was a devout and learned Christian; Cassin was knowledgeably cosmopolitan with regard to Western religious traditions; and Chang, although explicitly appealing to Confucian virtues, specifically "ren" and "li," in Article 1 of the UDHR, was clearly responsive to a more obvious notion of universal human equality. All four were cognizant of the indebtedness of liberal democratic principles to the Christian theological vision of humans as persons gifted with an inalienable dignity through created participation in the freedom and value of a transcendent God.

All four of them were finally content, however, and not only for reasons of political expediency, that this indebtedness should remain unarticulated in the UDHR. Why were they satisfied with the document's blunt and metaphysically unexplained assertion of human dignity as a contribution, and spur, to the cultural promotion of attention to dignity and rights? First, because they were all universalists, meaning they all believed that human nature was the same everywhere, and that therefore unfettered human reason would, in every culture, lead sooner or later to the same insights into equal, inherent human worth. Second, because they were all pluralists, meaning they believed that the truth about equal inherent human dignity could be equivalently symbolized in different languages in different cultures, and that such languages would reflect equivalent insights about dignity grounded in equivalent experiences adequately interpreted.

Was this confidence well founded? It is true that the original Jewish and Christian experiences that engendered insights into the human person as imago Dei yielded not only that symbol but also all the later elaborations of Christian theologizing with respect to the infinite value of each person. But it remains a question whether experiences and insights equivalent to these either have occurred or would—given the survival of the human race—eventually occur in major cultures around the world. It is a good question, if exceedingly difficult to speculate about convincingly, a speculation that would take us well off our own course. But a question constrained enough in scope to explore here is what the key drafters hoped might be the future political role of the UDHR's metaphysically noncontextualized idea of equal inherent dignity.

It seems that they regarded the bare—one might say abstracted—concept of inherent human dignity in the UDHR to be a strength rather than a weakness, because disengaging the concept from all religious and philosophical reference allows it to evoke the mystery of inherent human value in a universal and open-ended way. Decontextualization allows the idea of inherent human dignity to function as an *intrinsically heuristic concept*. What does this phrase mean?

Something is said to have a "heuristic" character when it serves and invites the effort of discovery. The x in an algebraic equation is a heuristic symbol, in that it stands for a mathematical content we do not yet know but aim to discover. Any word can be said to have a heuristic role as soon as it piques our curiosity through awareness that, even though we have some understanding of its meaning, our knowledge of that meaning is incomplete. Terms cease to function heuristically when we attain a satisfactorily complete understanding of them. For example, there may come a time when we can say we know with certainty the meaning of the term "habitat" or the term "voltage," since no further relevant questions reasonably arise with regard to our understanding of their basic definitions.

But some words signify concepts that are *intrinsically* heuristic, concepts whose meaning-content can always be more deeply grasped through further acts of knowing, where more discovery always remains possible, where further relevant questions always arise, where we know that the concept's meaning can never be understood completely or definitively by a human being. To say that a word signifies an intrinsically heuristic concept means that it refers to an intelligible reality of which we have some understanding, but whose full or complete meaning remains and will always to some degree remain unknown to us. Intrinsically heuristic concepts play a central role in human self-knowing. A good example is the concept of happiness as famously examined by Aristotle in the *Nicomachean Ethics*. Aristotle succeeds in filling in the meaning-content of the concept of human happiness to no small extent, but in the end, his analysis concludes that its meaning is not completely knowable by us.

Plato's dialogues at times entail the exploration of intrinsically heuristic concepts, such as justice, love, and courage. In the pertinent dialogues, some discovery about the notion under investigation takes place, but at dialogue's end there is never a declaration of having satisfactorily achieved a complete definition. Sometimes, there is an insistence that further examination can proceed only by way of exploring the "likely stories" of myth, since human stories are a participation in the supervening mystery of the divine story. On other occasions, dialogues end with the assertion that the exploration has gotten off-track, or indeed barely gotten underway. The dramas of important dialogues and their conclusions are structured in this way not merely because Plato wants his readers to think through matters for themselves, and to mature through a personal search for moral insight, though that is one of his aims. It is also because he knows that with regard to ideas such as justice, courage, love, and virtue, no complete understanding is available to human beings. But at the same time, the more understanding we do attain, the more our personal moral advance is possible, so that recurrent investigation, in good faith, is always desirable.

We can reasonably assert that the key drafters of the UDHR recognized that the notion of inherent human dignity can serve as an intrinsically heuristic concept, and were confident that presenting it as a bare, unexplained truth in the preamble and Article 1 would free it up to function as such. Sympathetic readers of the UDHR would accept, they will have decided, that inherent dignity is a meaningful, fact-based concept that invites further exploration, with some readers exploring it even to the point of discovering its historical foundations and philosophical implications.

CHAPTER FOURTEEN

Persons, Rights, and Dignified Living

The phrase "inherent human dignity" refers to the value of being a person. What is a person? Sometimes we hear impassioned assertions that it is unreasonably anthropocentric to ascribe personhood only to human beings, and that animals, too, should be considered persons, even plants. Maybe the earth itself, Gaia. Such arguments emerge largely from two convictions: (1) personhood should be ascribed to any being that is sentient in any manner or degree, or even, perhaps, to each biological organism, and (2) all beings are interconnected. To the first point, to ascribe personhood to any concrete manifestation of sentience or biological thing at any level of ontological development or complexity (e.g., a blade of grass, an oyster, a cat) is—however nobly motivated—philosophically wrongheaded, in that it ignores the results of thousands of years of efforts to understand human distinctiveness based on the full range of available data on human beings. To the second point, to argue for the importance of recognizing the ontological involvement of all beings with each other—on a bioregional, planetary, or universal scale—is of itself no more than a reminder of the oneness of the cosmos, which indeed we would always do well to remember.

But we also need to remember, when reflecting on the oneness of the cosmos, that each identifiable thing is both one with everything else that is *and* distinct from it. Distinguishing what it is that makes a type of thing just what it is, is the foundation of both philosophy and science. Some exuberant souls are ready to dismiss both philosophy and science, or to be more exact their perspectival legacies, as intrinsically misguided and harmful. It is unlikely that they will be reading this. Rocks are not plants, plants are not animals, and humans (though it sounds odd to modern ears) are ontologically distinct from animals, plants, and minerals.

Animal being is obviously the foundation of humanness. But in human beings, the general range of capacities belonging to the sensitive psyche of higher animals are brought into a higher functional integration (i.e., are depended upon, but guided beyond the scope of, their intrinsic capabilities; are "sublated," Hegel says) through the operations of human consciousness, operations whose presence as potential or as active make us human. The idea of "person" is an important element in any philosophical exposition of the fact that the absorption, or sublation, of animality into a higher unifying ontological sphere of spiritually cognitive purposiveness makes humans not just another species of animal, but a distinct *genus of being*, a distinct kind of "unity-identity-whole," to use Lonergan's terminology.[1]

One characteristic of this higher ontological sphere constituted by human conscious operations is *awareness* of being a limited participation in the ground of being, the ground that, when adequately understood, is recognized to be a space-and-time-transcending realm of meaning. One could say that human consciousness, manifesting as a person, is—in a primordial ontological sense—where transcendent reality reveals itself through individual human personhood, in the course of the latter revealing its personhood through being present with and present to other persons. Or one could say, a person is a site in worldly reality where an awareness of being simultaneously identical with and different from everything else—as a participation in the process of reality—is also an awareness of being a conscious participant in a transcendent realm of meaning in process of revelation *to oneself* by way of relationships *with other persons*.

What are the conscious operations that belong specifically to persons? They include, among other operations, (1) self-aware acts of inquiry (inquiry accompanied by awareness and by awareness of this awareness) into the various types of data presented by sensations, imaginings, feelings, and memory, as well as by the conscious operations of one's mind; (2) self-aware acts of conceptual understanding, knowing, and creating; (3) self-aware acts of free deciding and behaving, in the service of self-determining; and (4) self-aware acts of loving, both spontaneous and willed. The result is conscious human performance, the "operating" of personhood, which displays certain well-known attributes. For example, awareness of the responsibility that the exercise of freedom entails, and, through awareness of being a responsible shaper of one's personal identity, awareness of being unique and irreplaceable.

Accompanying this conscious performative artistry is an awareness of the capacity to suffer (physically and spiritually) and of all the fragilities of personhood. We recognize how easily our freedom to make or define ourselves is undermined, both by ourselves and by others; how often our desire to perform admirably in the drama of living is thwarted by our misconceptions and our biases, by the actions of others, and how our desire to understand and to love (and to be understood and loved) so often goes unmet.

The value of personhood thus described constitutes (more or less) the value of inherent human dignity affirmed in the UN Universal Declaration of Human Rights (UDHR). And human rights derive from this inherent value. It is because humans are capable of the operations involved in responsible self-making, and are unique and fragile beings, that we have "inalienable rights" to the conditions and opportunities that allow for our free and full development as persons, that is, that allow for the pursuit of dignified living. Dignified *living*, it is to be emphasized, is an *achievement*. In this, it differs categorically from inherent dignity, which is the idea that there is a value that every human being possesses innately and that is an unconditional given. Consequently, we must distinguish sharply between, on the one hand, the conditional respect accorded to persons on the basis of their exhibiting dignified choices, achievements, and manners of speech and deed, and, on the other hand, the unconditional respect owed to persons in their inherent value.

According to the UDHR, what are the rights whose recognition and institutionalization are most important for securing the pursuit of dignified living? Civil and political rights, such as the rights to liberty, privacy, equality before the law; freedom from discrimination based on race, color, language, nationality, sex, property, birth, or religion; freedom of movement; freedom to marry and form a family; freedom to own property; freedom of thought, expression, and practice of religion; and freedom of peaceful assembly and association. Also economic and cultural rights, such as the right to education; the right to work; the right to equal pay for equal work; the right to a standard of living adequate for proper health care; the right to rest and leisure; the right to participate in cultural life; and the right to share in the benefits of scientific advance. Thus the rights enumerated in the UDHR are precisely those that are "indispensable for [a person's] dignity and the free *development* of his personality" (Article 22; emphasis added).

Also indispensable to dignified existence, states the UDHR, is the acceptance of certain obligations. For since persons can flourish only if their rights are respected, each of us has "duties to the community" entailing "due recognition and respect for the rights and freedoms of others" (Article 29). Thus, a conscientious embrace of social obligations is essential to dignified living. The notion of achieved dignity is also, like that of inherent dignity, a notion that the UDHR presents heuristically, since the actualized particulars of dignified existence will be achieved through ongoing insights and self-defining decisions and actions made by persons within their specific biographical and historical situations, entailing in each case a unique intertwining of physical and interpersonal circumstances, embedded in specific economic, technological, and cultural conditions.

What damage is done to a person's inherent dignity if he or she chooses to live in a ruinously undignified way? None at all. The failure to *achieve* dignified existence (leaving aside here any discussion of the criteria used to assess dignified living, and simply acknowledging that persons can choose to apply their freedom to determine themselves in disastrously inhuman, or unspiritual, ways) doesn't alter the intrinsic value given with personhood as such. Inherent human dignity is inviolable. It can't be destroyed by any means—not by others, nor by ourselves in our indifference, self-disgust, spiritual rebellion, or despair.

It remains present, too, in victims of torture or terrorism, even if it produces profound self-humiliation, a state of being reduced in one's own eyes to something less than human. It remains in persons who do evil by choice or by derangement. Admirable accomplishment and useful social function do not improve it; disastrous psychological conditions do not diminish it. And according to the UDHR—and all the conventions, constitutions, and jurisprudence that it has inspired and influenced—every person is equal in the possession of this unalterable inherent dignity.

What an idea! The most repellent, evil persons in the world, as transparencies for the divine personhood in which they participate, however vilely they have mismanaged this participation and have deformed or perverted the possibilities of character, are still each of infinite value. This is an idea that makes no sense, of course, unless one carefully distinguishes the equal inherent value that all humans share, by virtue of being human, from the existential value that a person develops (or destroys) in accordance with their degree of attunement with the divine love and goodness that grounds human participation in the cosmos.

CHAPTER FIFTEEN

Digression

The Universal Search for Dignified Living

Most people have not reflected systematically on the idea of their own inherent dignity—what exactly it consists of, and why it is inviolable. Even fewer have taken the trouble to consider why this inherent worth makes all human beings equal to each other. And fewer still have concerned themselves with the fact that equal inherent dignity presumes human participation in transcendent value. On the other hand, since an elementary awareness of one's value in being a person is intrinsic to human self-consciousness, every mature individual has a desire to live in a way that resonates with that awareness, and so has developed some ideas about what achieving a dignified existence entails. And we recognize too, of course, that human beings develop wildly varying conjectures regarding the matter. Individuals are motivated and drawn forward by these ideas about how existence is best managed—ideas associated with images linked to powerful feelings—because every person seeks not only to feel that their existence is meaningful, Viktor Frankl has famously explained,[1] but also seeks to feel that their living is *dignified*.

Any sufficiently rich account of human existence indicates how the different pursuits that can dominate a life serve the purpose of filling personal consciousness not only with a sense of meaningfulness but also a sense of *estimableness*. For example, striving for maximum pleasure (either gross or refined; see Kierkegaard's portrayal of "aesthetic existence" in the first volume of *Either/Or*), or the longing for security above all things, or the struggle to attain wealth and power, or a hunger for knowledge in matters practical or speculative, or efforts to achieve a life of virtue as exemplified by cultural heroes (or family members).

This is because we all sense that human existence is, Voegelin says, "participation in a movement with a direction to be found or missed," and no one, in fact, wants to miss the path of meaning and value, no one wants to feel pointless.[2] Lonergan makes the same point by saying that our overriding concern in life is a "dramatic" concern: we desire to turn in a performance that is admirable, even at its best beautiful, but one that at the very least doesn't seem, to ourselves or to others, ridiculous and hollow.[3]

Our performances in life are a matter of putting our freedom into play. We cherish our freedom, we glory in it, and we use it to make our lives feel purposeful and estimable (that is to say, dignified). This shaping of our lives is a kind of artistry, since art is, among other things, an exploration of the possible uses of human freedom — in this case, of the possibilities of what a concrete human existence (myself, this I) can be. Hegel described Shakespeare's greatest characters as being "free artists of themselves," and this is to some extent what we all are.[4] The search to achieve a dignified existence is a search to attain and sustain artistically manifested dignity in the performance of living. The assertion that this search for dignity applies to human beings universally may well elicit a skeptical response.

There appear to be two principal objections. First, it may be pointed out that many people engage in lifestyles and pursue goals that can hardly be described as dignified in any normal sense of the word. The appropriate answer to this is that every person identifies what is attractive in living with spontaneous or habitual objects of desire, that these objects of desire are imagined in terms of varied "acquisitions and attainments" (Lonergan), and that the acquisitions and attainments that a person associates with meaningful and dignified living can reflect a longing imagination that is immature, damagingly limited by circumstances, benighted, perverse, shot through with resentments (conscious and unconscious), or riddled with biases.[5] In other words, there are—to judge in comparison with the achieved dignity of the most virtuous of persons (Aristotle called them *spoudaioi*, morally serious persons, or men of good character[6])—a large variety of mistaken or shallow notions of dignified living that effectively inspire and inform much human performance.

In contemporary culture, consumerist greed, vanity-stoked hedonism, and a fascination with and longing to "touch" celebrity are some of the drives frequently absorbed and adopted as the stuff that makes existence charmed and worth living. In considering the universality of the search for achieved dignity, we need to recognize that here, once more, *dignity* functions as a heuristic notion. In this context, dignity considered as achieved dignity can be heuristically defined as "that which a person aims to artistically manifest through free performative choices."

There is a second, more radical objection to accepting that the search for dignified living universally characterizes human existence. This objection calls attention to the not infrequent human indulgence in, and enjoyment of, self-debasement and self-degradation. People can—and some do—take satisfaction in humiliating their own thirst for esteem, in ridiculing and lacerating their own longing for truth and goodness, in reviling and attacking their own sense of worth. To recognize how even this can be understood to be a form of the search for dignified living requires both dialectical subtlety and a sense of irony.

Friedrich Nietzsche, a master dialectician and ironist, provides a helpful clue as to how we might proceed. One of the epigrams in his *Beyond Good and Evil* states: "Whoever despises himself still respects himself as one who despises."[7] This insight is transposable to our own topic in this manner: "Whoever degrades himself still respects himself as one who degrades." And it is not difficult to identify in what this higher "himself" consists, the self who is still respected as the one choosing its own degradation. It is the self as freedom.

We can indulge, even revel, in the creative freedom we have to attack and debase our own inherent value. Sometimes this is done to violate or dishonor the awareness of inherent dignity because one feels strongly that the conceptions one has absorbed of what is involved in living up to it—the images called to mind by discussions and teachings about appropriate behavior and worthwhile living— have been imposed on one, so that any existential striving to conform to those images is associated with hypocrisy and a failure of personal authenticity. Self-harmful behavior of adolescents who in this manner display a vehement rejection of parental expectations is an everyday example of this. On a broader scale, consider historical situations where a conquering society's ideals of dignified living, imposed on conquered subjects, are profoundly alien to the conquered society's notions of dignified living. Within the conquered group, the choices of some persons to corrupt what is felt to be their own inherent value might be an understandable act of existential revolt. Sometimes engaging in self-degradation is chosen in order to outrage the sacred source of human dignity, out of indignation that personal freedom ontologically depends on the freedom of a transcendent ground, on the mysterious transcendent reality that has given to each human consciousness its freedom by way of participation.

Such intentional outrage is possible because human freedom really is free, but not self-granted. It is a real independence. And it can be felt that the only sure way, the only convincing way, of proving to oneself that one really *is* free is to reject not only what is socially expected but to reject the transcendent goodness and meaningfulness that is felt or understood to oblige one's own freedom.

Dostoevsky has explored this topic with remarkable discernment. The character of Kirillov, in *The Demons* (aka *The Possessed*), rejects the obligation of his freedom to a transcendent source (God), and concludes that the only way to successfully prove his independence from it is by freely eliminating his own free existence through suicide. At the limit of an existential living out of this rejection (that is, nonsuicidally), we find the Sadean persuasion. De Sade's novels vividly and compulsively dramatize the conviction that human beings can only have real—truly independent—worth if they thoroughly repudiate life as participation in a transcendent Good through enacting a continual, violently energetic degradation of self and others. In all these examples, what is occurring is always a self's exalting of its own freedom through self-degrading rebellion against the transcendent origin of value to which humans are existentially obliged for their freedom.

All lives focused on self-degradation, in the end, can be rightly understood as belonging to an intelligible subset of efforts to achieve a sufficiently self-constitutive existential performance, and therefore as warped but real examples of the universal search for dignified living.

CHAPTER SIXTEEN

The Challenge of Respecting Inherent Dignity

If inherent human dignity exists, then each person's contingent, historical particularity (embodied, fragile, transient) is also a participation in transcendent value, in an absolute and eternal good. The judgment that inherent dignity does exist coheres with the advocacy of liberal democracy, for the vision of the rightness of liberal democratic government presumes that all "are created equal," and a fact of inherent human dignity establishes ontologically a truth of human equality.

The logic of this last clause is fairly simple: there is no equal elementary value of persons if there is no transcendent value in which all humans participate and that each human presence incarnates. What else besides the showing-forth of a mystery of transcendent value in each person could the affirmation of the equality of all persons mean? That is, a true equality that can't be physically or psychologically observed or measured but that also is immune to violation, cannot be revoked by society, and that consists not only of equality before the law but entails an ontological equality. To respect equal inherent dignity in a philosophically and historically informed way means to respect every human being—including oneself—as a showing-forth of transcendent reality.

Those who understand this about themselves can get sidetracked in their excitement about it. We often see this in religious people who hold firm to the fact of human involvement in transcendence but—alas!—forget or deny the *mysteriousness* of both the transcendent ground and of self-aware participation in it. Such cases manifest problems with regard to both experiential openness and self-interpretation.

Those who attend with proper experiential openness to the mysteriousness of the transcendent Beyond (whatever their relationship to religion or spiritual practice) recognize that the within of consciousness reveals *boundlessness*, or "illocality," Emily Dickinson once wrote.[1] Two and a half millennia before Dickinson, Heraclitus had already stated, "You will not find out the limits of the soul by going, even if you travel over every way, so deep is its *logos*."[2] Philo, five centuries after Heraclitus: "Those who can see lift their eyes to heaven, and contemplate the Manna, the divine Logos. Those who cannot see, look at the onions in the ground."[3] Nothing against onions or gardening. It's a metaphor. The contemplation of boundlessness tends to put a damper on smug religious certitude and mania.

Those who *do* recognize the mystery of the transcendent Beyond, though, still all too easily fall into the self-interpretative trap of thinking that it is only a person's "spirit," and not also the animalic level of being together with its underlying manifolds of subanimalic processes—all of which are elements of the unity-identity-whole that is a human being—that has intrinsic value. But it is the whole human being—in its incarnate unity—that possesses inherent dignity. Every human person is embodied: physical, chemical, and complex biological structures make possible and sustain personal being-in-the-world, and every embodied person is an ontological unity. Inherent dignity therefore accrues, in a human being, to each level in the hierarchy of being sustaining a personal presence. Inherent dignity reaches down through all the building blocks of a human life.

This is why achievements of dignified living are not necessary for inherent dignity to be manifest. Inherent dignity shows itself in the entire human being, whatever that human being does, might do, or cannot do. It remains true that the notion of inherent human dignity arose from appreciation of the distinctive (spiritual) capacities that belong to normally functioning humans, including the capacities of self-aware inquiry and insight, self-aware moral choice, self-aware creativity and love, and the complex conscious artistry of self-determination. But any of these capacities might be diminished, damaged, not yet effective, or only formerly effective, all while a person's *humanness* is still being manifest, is still "there," in which case inherent dignity is still "there." Damian Fedoryka has stated the matter with precision: "Dignity is predicated [on the fact] of the being itself rather than any of its specific properties, even if these properties are the reason that dignity is predicated."[4]

What, then, is the most elementary human presentation that should call forth our basic respect for human dignity? Simply the living human being in his or her physical presence, a presence that represents all the potentialities of a human being as free, rational, moral, self-defining, and loving even when the effective probabilities of realizing these potentialities are in the individual case low, minimal, or—as far as we can tell—zero, and even when free self-making has become degraded and twisted.

Emmanuel Levinas has written that this presence confronts us most inescapably through the human face. That which is presented in the human face, he says, "visits me as already ab-solute," that is, as nondissolvable into bare matter, or into a mere means to an end.[5] The face turns to me, beseeching or angry, inquisitive or indifferent, eloquent or mute. But in every case, it remains a window onto transcendence, and so inherent dignity makes its claim on me. And we note: any part of the human body can *represent* the face—a hand, a bony kneecap. I can respect this inherent dignity, or I can turn away.

And if I do not "turn away"? What does this mean, existentially speaking? It means respecting the inherent dignity of the person by willing their good (to whatever degree this willing is actualized—perhaps only as a fleeting attitude of concern). To "will the good of the other," this is one of the classic definitions of "love" in Western philosophy. Love in this sense obviously doesn't mean (merely) a certain type of emotion, or a propulsive experience of *eros*, but it's not something incompatible with either of them. Here "love" means a self-transcending concern for the well-being of a creature. That creature may be oneself. To love oneself, in the higher sense, means to will one's own good: the good, say, of being virtuous, or authentic, or healthy. And it is a self-transcending concern for the well-being of oneself, a self-transcending relationship to oneself being possible because of self-presence, which allows one to stand, as it were, aside from oneself (from the Latin roots, *ex* = "out of," and *sisto, sistere* = "stand": "stand out of") and engage in self-choosing. So we can despise ourselves, be indifferent to ourselves, be greedy for ourselves, or—in a joyful and virtuous sense—love ourselves.

To will the good of a person, through the act of being respectful of their inherent dignity, always has implications for one's relationship to transcendence, since every person is a transparency for the transcendent ground of being. To be loving toward anyone with respect to their inherent human value is at the same time to calibrate one's relationship with the ontological absolute that (though remaining mysterious) grounds the absoluteness of inherent human dignity.

Of course, it's often difficult to respect the inherent dignity of a particular person. Consider the case of a terrorist. On July 22, 2011, the Norwegian domestic terrorist Anders Behring Breivik, a far-right ideologue, detonated a bomb in downtown Oslo, killing eight people, and shortly afterward on the island of Utoya shot to death sixty-nine participants in a Worker's Youth League summer camp. Once he was captured, on Utoya, and his responsibility for his actions readily admitted by him, why was he not simply executed on the spot? Because, on the basis of his inherent dignity as a human being, he was regarded as having rights, including a right to be free of extralegal punishment, a right to trial by jury, a right to the opportunity for self-explanation, and a right to respectful treatment in court.

So, Anders Breivik, even after his murder of seventy-seven people, was still regarded by lawful authorities in a liberal democracy to have an intrinsic human worth of incalculable value. Not only that. The principle of human equality affirms that the inherent personhood of Breivik, the condemned and incarcerated terrorist (Norway has no death penalty) remains as "deserving of reverence" (to use Kant's phrase) as does any other human being.[6] Breivik, an anti-Islamist and anti-immigrationist, who stated that he was acting to defend Christian Europe, would obviously find laughable any idea of human equality, including the idea of persons being of equal value insofar as they are self-aware participants in a transcendent ground of the cosmos.

Persons, for Breivik, are not equals, even in this radical (root) sense. As this shows, respecting universal inherent dignity has its grim ironies. For in the wake of an act of terror, the perpetrator must be regarded as still imbued with the "sacredness of the person" (Hans Joas) that—considered simply in terms of personhood—remains no less sacred than that of his victims.[7]

None of this is to suggest, of course, that the views or actions of terrorists are dignified, worthy of respect. Respect for a person's choices or manner of living, for what he or she existentially achieves or becomes, is conditional. But the inherent dignity even of villains is inviolable, and therefore demands, however much it might discomfit us, a certain unconditional respect.

CHAPTER SEVENTEEN

Transcendent Mystery and Shakenness

Those committed to truths of inherent human dignity and inalienable rights may, or may not, focus their concern specifically on the transcendence of the absolute value that validates these truths. If they do, they may decide that it is fruitless to ponder this transcendence, since the essence of transcendent reality lies, by definition, beyond all that human participatory knowing can experience, understand, or say. What would be best, they may decide, is to acknowledge the fact of it to oneself—perhaps avoiding, as the UN Universal Declaration of Human Rights (UDHR) does, any metaphysical or religious elaborating—and then turn attention to the social and political work of securing or shoring up recognition of dignity and rights. In such a way people can affirm that there is a transcendent reality without this acknowledgment becoming for them an existential difficulty.

But it may be argued—Kierkegaard did famously—that if the truth of this transcendent absolute is *not* existentially embraced and grappled with as a difficulty, one is not really affirming transcendence at all. For, Kierkegaard would say, as soon as transcendence has become just another fact, it has lost its living truth. The argument here is that any real relationship with transcendent reality must entail ongoing conscious existential effort in the face of uncertainties: uncertainty about substantive meaning of transcendent reality, uncertainty as to why there is a cosmos of which it is the ground, and uncertainty about the ultimate purpose of one's own existence, since existence is one's participation in the cosmos and its ground. If this is the case, then engaging in a real, personal, inward affirmation of transcendence involves a certain existential drama.

The twentieth-century Czech philosopher Jan Patočka has described this drama in the following fashion. Everyday existence, he says, typically takes refuge in embracing life in the world as *essentially nonproblematic*. That is, humans normally accept a host of culturally established foundational truths about the meaning of existence as given and as certain. Many existentially important problems have to be dealt with as one navigates living, perhaps starting with whether or not to take moral values seriously. But rarely do people question matters all the way down to first principles—to the point where it is impossible to evade the fact that the cosmic ground is most pronouncedly a Mystery, which is also the point where the why's and wherefore's of one's bewildering relationship to this Mystery come into focus and thus become problematic.

If a person does reach the point where he or she radically questions received givens and certitudes concerning the cosmic ground and our human relationship to it, there inevitably follows a certain degree of emotional and intellectual liberation from ordinary, familiar routines of existential perception and orientation. But this is achieved, Patočka writes, only through anxious discovery that the core of such "open" existence (existence in relation to a problematic cosmic ground) is an unsettling "spirit of free meaning bestowal."[1] What does this mean?

With the phrase "free meaning bestowal," Patočka is not suggesting that a person, by way of such openness to the ground of reality as problematic, discovers that "meaning" is merely a human invention, or that reality is whatever a person decides it to be. Rather, he is alluding to an experience in which culturally absorbed pregiven certitudes about the ground of the cosmos (certitudes such as "the gods and goddesses we have worshipped for as long as we can remember are the basis of reality," or "the ground of reality is the biblical God," or "the divinities of Creator, Sustainer, and Destroyer together best symbolize the transcendent realm beyond human imagination," or "the ground of being is whatever 'energy' turns out to be when, finally, it is understood mathematically") are *disrupted*—so that the Question that is human existence, along with any cultural answers, undergoes what Patočka calls an elementary "shaking," a "shaking of life" through a shaking of "naively accepted meaning."[2]

In such an experience, radical questioning dissolves not only all previously conceived and imagined answers concerning the ground of the cosmos, but (this is key) all *knowable* answers. It discloses that the ground of being is, in its essence, permanently mysterious—a Beyond that truly lies beyond all efforts of human knowing and beyond spatiotemporal being—to which the "shaken" soul must remain, in order to be authentically affirming it, in a relationship of *perpetual questioning*, which is not, however, a state of affective, cognitive, and imaginal cluelessness. One is still, after all, in relationship with a ground of reality to which one knows one ultimately belongs, and toward which one is, as a human inquirer and knower, anticipatorily oriented by all sorts of clues.[3]

In such a "shaken but undaunted" posture of inquiry, a person comes to realize three things: (1) that the ground of reality is indeed a realm of meaning, but meaning that is in itself an abyss of mystery; (2) that this ontological source of the capacity of one's own personal freedom to bestow as-yet-only-possible meanings, as one navigates existence, is a dizzying "no-thing" consisting of the radically transcendent freedom and value belonging to the ground; and (3) that the participation of one's personal understanding, freedom, creating, and loving in this mystery of the transcendent ground is human (and spiritual) existence.[4] Perhaps to understate the obvious: not everyone is willing to sustain the recurrent existential openness to ultimate uncertainties involved in such a "shaking."

In Patočka's view, it is not to be expected that what Václav Havel called the "general human experience of the absolute" will produce in many people—much less universally—an appreciation of the fact that words so unthreatening as "the unconditioned" and "the transcendent" are actually, in their historical and existential origins, intimately related to shaken experiences of a cosmic abyss of mystery.[5] Yet these are the experiential origins of *living* notions of transcendence, experiences testified to by countless mystics, philosophers, prophets, artists, and saints, East and West, over the course of millennia.

Once a person grasps the validity of such experiences, it becomes impossible to ignore that in the human comprehension of the process of reality there lies a core of both existential ignorance and of linguistic incapacity. To appreciate that we participate in a transcendent abyss of mystery means understanding, first, that this mystery "incomprehensibly lies beyond all that we experience of it in participation," and second, that it can be spoken of, or artistically represented, "only by characterizing it as reaching beyond all symbolic language" (Voegelin).[6] To state this in positive terms: a person in this posture of appreciation now definitely *knows* that humans participate in a ground of reality that can never under the conditions of worldly existence be fully understood, and *knows* that the content of this ground can never be adequately represented in speech, music, art. "Shaken openness to transcendence" alters the conscious negotiating of our being-in-the-world. It entails relinquishing a presumption of cognitive mastery over the ground of meaning—a presumption that, in typical everydayness, we never consciously decided upon but rather absorbed unconsciously as we imbibed cultural givens regarding reality. How could it be otherwise than that, when young, each of us found elementary existential balance by unthinkingly accepting basic assumptions regarding the Whole of reality and its ground, including, in antispiritual cultures or families, that the Whole is all that is immanent? That is, the totality of physical things and their properties? This openness and shakenness alter the character of our relationships with other people.

For when I discover that the essence of my existence is participation in the value of a transcendent absolute, I find also, on the basis of how I now relate to this and that person who has become, Buber says, a Thou for me, that *all* persons are participants in the infinite value of the absolute, and therefore that each person is both infinitely precious and constantly vulnerable, which means that my responsibility to each person is also infinite. What is an infinite responsibility to other persons? It is a responsibility that has no boundaries, no limits, and no excuses. Of course, it is impossible for me to fully live up to such a responsibility (see Dostoyevsky on the topic). But I can acknowledge it. And do my best.

Finally, this shaking of life reveals to me that some others have undergone a similar experience of disruption, have indeed remained open to a recurrent "shaking" disruption through holding onto uncertainties about the ground of being. Most of these I meet in the pages of books, or through art; a few, perhaps, I meet face to face. Thus, a community of the "shaken but undaunted" comes into view, a community established (Patočka insists) on a unique solidarity: "the solidarity of the shaken."[7] Some members of this community of the shaken, certainly, have been or will be inclined toward a commitment to equal inherent human dignity and human rights, but not all of them. This is because not all of them will have experienced the transcendent ground as a Thou, and the logic of the idea of equal inherent dignity and equal inalienable rights requires that the transcendent Mystery revealed in existential openness be encountered as a transcendent Thou—a Mystery of Personhood.

And even this is not sufficient. For the idea of inherent dignity follows, historically and existentially, from recognition that the transcendent God whose impenetrable Mystery induces such shakenness is representatively present, as absolute value, *in every person*—male and female, Jew and Gentile, rich and poor, moral beacon and moral bankrupt. In sum: those united in a solidarity of the shaken will be inclined to affirm equal inherent dignity when transcendence as a Mystery of Personhood has drawn witness, further, to a Mystery of Incarnation.

CHAPTER EIGHTEEN

Eclipsing Transcendent Mystery

There is a well-known way to prevent transcendent mystery from becoming a living truth, and to keep uncertainties about the ground of reality—and existential shakenness—at bay. It is to assure oneself that no such uncertainties exist. Despite the fact that human consciousness, whose basis is an unrestricted questioning, is inherently oriented toward the recognition of the mystery of the ground of being—along with the mystery of the meaning of moral striving and the mystery of the outcome of history—it is possible to replace that orientation with one of two forms of ultimate certitude: religious certitude or antispiritual certitude. In both cases, the narrative completeness of meaning that is the cosmos has apparently ceased to be mysterious. The whole story is presumed to be known.

It is always salutary to recall that, as participants who have emerged within the Whole, we can in fact only ever have a perspectival understanding of the cosmos. How tempting it is to assume that because we are *knowing* participants within this Whole, and know *of* it and know *some* of the realities belonging to it, that we can know *all about* it. First, there is religious presumption of certitude about ultimates. This is manifest in those who claim to be in possession of definitive answers concerning, for example, the being and will of

God, the afterlife, how to achieve perfect attunement with ultimate reality, or the future and final outcome of history. Such presumption does grant consciousness its awareness of the fact of transcendent reality, but it betrays the mysteriousness of the transcendent realm of meaning. And that betrayal changes everything. A religious person who presumes absolute and essentially complete knowledge of the ground and of the Whole—a "knowing," a *gnosis*, that replaces genuine faith, love, hope, and trust, and the appreciations and insights that support and belong to these—cannot but involve a corruption of his own nature. Somewhere along the line, he substitutes a comforting fantasy for authentic vision, or, at the least, adds fantasy to authentic spiritual vision. Religious certitude, in its most virulent and vehement modes, can lead to wars of religion, wars we still live with. The fifteenth-century Indian mystic Kabir stated his sardonic view of the matter: "The Hindu says / Rama's dear to him, / The Muslim says it's Rahim. / They go to war / and kill each other."[1]

Second, there is the secular counterpart to the religious mystery-resisters. Antispiritual "owners of ultimate truth" are certain both that there is no transcendent or divine reality and that human mastery of ultimate meanings has already been achieved either as already-known facts or as procedural methods that will yield complete and final answers. The latter is the province of scientific and technocratic partisans who wave off symbols of transcendent mystery as irrelevancies or delusions. Such owners of ultimate truth also include political activists who are certain not only that the perfecting of human society is possible but that they know how to reach this goal. These latter—let's call them "activists of certitude"—are well exemplified by Lenin and other leaders of the Bolshevik Revolution. They were confident that they already knew the essentials of the entire story of human history: where it's going, how it ends, a story identical, in their view, with the narrative completeness of meaning that is the cosmos, on the presumption that reality consists only of *material being*, and that this material being reaches its utmost achievement (development, realization) in human life.

And what was the goal of historical development according to the prophets and guides of Bolshevism? Salvation. The Bolsheviks promised salvation from evils that had always been endemic to human existence, such as injustice, social and political oppression, class conflict, economic exploitation, poverty and hunger, and warfare. They proclaimed that it was on the basis of certain, scientific knowledge of how to secure this salvation—and, indeed, the freedom and well-being of all humanity—that they overthrew the existing order in Russia.

These historical and ideological facts are familiar enough. But why, we may ask, did the Bolshevik Revolution with its goals of universal human well-being exhibit from the very beginning—not later on in Soviet society, as we often hear, but from its very first days—a thoroughgoing assault on the notion of the value of the individual person? Why did it pronounce disdain for the principle of personal dignity? And contempt for the sanctity of human life? The answer seems obvious once certain facts are linked together. The Bolshevik doctrines pronounced (in accordance with Marxist principles) that "God" is an illusion, that religion teaches only falsehoods (because all reality is material being), that there are no mysteries of transcendent meaning or transcendent value, that classes and social hierarchies are evil since all persons are equal, and that Bolshevik guidance will achieve the societal realization of human equality.

A historically and philosophically informed understanding of the idea of "the equality of persons," however, grasps not only that this idea originated in spiritual experiences and insights but that its meaning is essentially spiritual. Persons may be regarded as equal insofar as each possesses an incalculable, inherent value (dignity) through participating in, and being transparent for, the absolute of transcendent value. Absent of such participation in transcendent value, persons could have no inherent, inviolable, equal value. What could an equality of purely material human beings even mean? Equality shown through what material measurements?

Likewise, unless through participation in transcendent value each individual possesses incalculable value, no value could inhere in personal *uniqueness*. Thus it is not a surprise to find the eclipse of the mystery of God in Bolshevik rhetoric, and ideas informing Soviet policies, to be joined closely with the eclipse of the intrinsic value of unique personal existence, with the worth of human beings, instead, evaluated solely on the basis of their productive capacities as "natural resources" (Alexander Yakovlev).[2]

Denunciation of the intrinsic value of individual persons pervaded Bolshevik culture and permeated its application of the "world's routine of power" (to borrow a phrase from the poet Geoffrey Hill).[3] This was manifested in a disdain for the most elementary principle of the liberal democratic tradition: that individuals have a right to life. Many comments by Lenin and other Bolshevik leaders could be quoted to the purpose, but a comment of Leon Trotsky's—which unites contempt for the value of the individual per se with contempt for religion—represents their shared attitude: "We must put an end once and for all," he wrote to Lenin, "to the papist-Quaker babble about the sanctity of human life."[4] The idea of the intrinsic value of the individual was for Trotsky an irrelevant nuisance that clouds the recognition that human destiny concerns only *the mass of society* conceived as a material, unitary whole.

In Bolshevik education, therefore, an ideological substitute had to be found for the West's civilizational teachings—intricately elaborated over millennia—that a human being's authentic relationship to moral truths is rooted in his or her *personal* insights, and that *personal* conscientiousness and decision-making are at the core of moral destiny. A human being could no longer be morally assessed on the basis of being a unique person who thinks or does right or wrong, but only in an impersonal manner: on the assumption that each human being is nothing more than "an atom" of the material labor force that is to be "judged, reorganized, redistributed" by state powers (Rosenstock-Huessy).[5] Morality ceased to have any metaphysical or spiritual meaning; it was interpreted solely with regard to practical utility, and utility was defined in statist terms.

Lenin summed up the matter this way: "Everything that contributes to the building of a Communist society is moral, everything that hinders it is immoral."[6] Suddenly everything was permitted if the act or process was considered socially useful. People became *matériel* for the society coming into being through revolutionary guidance and activity. Human worth was the perceived contribution to state aims and goals.

The consequence? Adding up state-ordered (often extralegal) executions, deaths in labor camps, deaths in the suppression of peasant revolts, deaths resulting from the state-organized terror-famine in Ukraine in the early 1930s, deaths caused by forced relocations of ethnic communities and "undesirables" to almost-uninhabitable regions of the country, and executions of repatriated prisoners of war following World War II, it has been estimated conservatively that the Bolshevik/Soviet system was responsible for the murder of at least 60 million of its citizens.[7]

This is an unusually grand-scale example, of course, of what can happen when activists of certitude manage to take charge of human affairs. But that doesn't keep it from serving as an example relevant to every scale, down to the most minor political instance, of how the principles of inherent dignity, inalienable rights, and human equality can become vulnerable when an antispiritual eclipse of transcendent mystery takes hold.

CHAPTER NINETEEN

Inherent Dignity as Both Concept and Mythic Symbol

Herman Melville's novel *Moby Dick* appeared in 1851. In one of its now-celebrated passages, the narrator expounds on the democratic principle of equal human dignity, linking it to the Christian vision of God's presence in every person, a vision of the "divine equality" that gives the democratic principle its meaning and validity:

> Men may seem detestable as joint stock-companies and nations; knaves, fools, and murderers there may be; men may have mean and meagre faces; but man, in the ideal, is so noble and so sparkling, such a grand and glowing creature, that over any ignominious blemish in him all his fellows should run to throw their costliest robes.... [T]his august dignity I treat of, is not the dignity of kings and robes, but that abounding dignity which has no robed investiture. [It is] that democratic dignity which, on all hands, radiates without end from God; Himself! The great God absolute! The centre and circumference of all democracy! His omnipresence, our divine equality![1]

Suppose someone were to read this passage and, being reminded of famous assertions (such as that in the UN Universal Declaration of Human Rights [UDHR]) that all humans are equal in sharing an inherent dignity, were to ask, "What exactly *is* this dignity, universal and invisible, that validates the ideal of democratic government? And furthermore, is this just an attractive and popular idea, or is it really true that everyone (myself included) possesses this special value that makes us all equal?"

The first question seeks understanding of the intelligibility of the idea of inherent dignity; its answer, as no more than an *idea*, will be a hypothetical with respect to *truth*. It calls for insight and conceptual clarification, but these carry no necessary existential significance for the questioner. The second question, however, asks whether or not the idea refers to a *fact*, and thus is existentially charged, because if the answer to the second question is yes, then the result will be that the inquirer affirms as true something that has major consequences for how he or she should live, regard others, and understand his situation in the cosmos.

A satisfactory answer to the first question may be arrived at by examining monographs and anthologies of essays on the idea of human dignity, of which there are a multitude. What would come into focus is something like the pattern of ideas presented in my chapter 11: inherent dignity is a concept, rooted in the *imago Dei* tradition, that refers to the distinctive value of human beings because of their capacities of rational thought, the moral exercise of freedom, creativity, love, self-determination, and the uniqueness of each person. This dignity is a given of human existence that is inviolable and irrevocable, originating in an absolute of transcendent value in which each personal existence participates.

It will be discovered, too, that the idea of inherent dignity that has emerged in Western modernity is fully intelligible—finally coheres—only when one takes into account an implicit context of Christian anthropological insights (a fact understood by the key drafters of the UDHR). These insights might be adumbrated (using some phrases of Voegelin's) as follows.

To claim the absolute spiritual equality of all persons is to claim, first, that a human being is human "insofar as he is *imago Dei*," and then more specifically that this "image of God" has been revealed to be what it truly is through the Christian *mythoi* telling the story of a personal Creator-God whose incarnation in history has revealed, with radical originality, that each individual is an equally beloved, equally valuable embodiment of divine presence in history.[2] That is, the "symbolism of the Incarnation," the vision of God becoming flesh at a concrete time in history, communicates—to those who understand its implications—that the existential representation of divine presence in history has been articulated down to the level of *each individual person*.[3] The meanings of these Christian *mythoi* are no less integral to the idea of inherent dignity (and thus of human equality) than the nonmythic ideas, readily embraced in modernity, of distinctive human capabilities of self-determination, rational thought, moral freedom, love, and creativity.

The meanings packed into Melville's passage should now make sense. The idea of inherent dignity that informs the democratic vision of equality becomes clear through a set of insights that combine various concepts pertaining to human nature and human participation in a transcendent absolute with various mythic symbols at the heart of the Christian tale of humanity's participation in God. Upon attaining this set of insights, our inquirer will no longer be in the dark about the basic meaning of the idea of inherent dignity that is ubiquitous in modern political discourse, but he will suspect that many people who publicly use the term don't have a very clear understanding of what it means.

Let us now imagine that our inquirer takes up the second question: Is this idea true? Does everyone (himself included) really possess this inherent dignity? To answer this with an affirmation—yes, it is true—requires the discovery that there is sufficient evidence to reasonably make this claim. Where is this evidence to be found? Not in any observable human behavior. The data constituting evidence for affirming as true that every person has an inherent dignity—whose foundation is the confirmation of the inquirer's *own* inherent dignity—will be discovered principally in the data of the inquirer's own consciousness, in his experiences of interpersonal relations, and in the teachings and literature of certain religious and philosophical traditions.

To start with, there may be found sufficient evidence to affirm that one reasons and knows, that one can freely decide to perform morally good actions, that one has to some degree shaped one's own character, that one has been a creator (at least in the self-artistry of dramatic living), that one has loved, does love, and is loved, and that one is a unique individual. Affirming these as facts, the inquirer can state that it is true, simply by virtue of being a human being, that I have the value—dignity—of being a rational, moral, free, creative, unique, and loving creature.

But why judge this value to be *incalculable*, a worth incommensurate with all worldly "price," as Kant proclaims, an *infinite* value, making all human beings equal in their basic infinite worth?[4] Here one begins to broach topics that a secularist would sidestep, the first being the fact of ontological derivation of each self from a ground of being whose substance, or essence, is beyond our knowing. The truth of equal inherent dignity presupposes this derivation, even though by itself the truth of this derivation of human existence from a transcendent ground doesn't suffice to establish human equality. (See, for example, Hindu religion regarding *atman* and *Brahman*, and the seeming unshakeability of Hindu class structure.) And though a secularist hesitates here, there is really nothing about this judgment of human derivation from a mysterious ground that requires the embrace of religious *mythoi*. Indeed, much about one's involvement in the ground of being can be established as facts for which evidence is available either through direct experience or rational deduction from direct experience. This includes one's knowledge that one is a *derived* being, that the source of one's being must have the character of transcendence, since spiritual (i.e., nonphysical) qualities cannot be accounted for on the basis of phenomena that belong to intrinsically material levels of being, that one's relationship with the transcendent ground is one of participation, and that to this ground, ontologically speaking, one ultimately belongs.

But if one proceeds to commit oneself to *equal inherent dignity* as a truth, this in the end *does* require that one commit oneself also in an affirming relationship to certain *mythoi*, specifically, to certain Christian *mythoi* concerning transcendence and our human involvement in it. In the end, this commitment takes one beyond both directly experienced evidence and rational deductions deriving from such evidence. It entails the existential risk of accepting as valid a number of likely stories about God, and the purposes of human existence that have been passed down and elaborated in the Christian tradition, an acceptance that is a matter of reasoned faith (or informed belief). These "truths of faith" will not present themselves as *arbitrary* truths, for they will be *mythoi* that suggest themselves as the *most likely* truths about transcendence and human participation in it because of their concordance with what can confidently be known about key *existentialia* through rational judgment on the basis of evidence provided by one's own consciousness and by interpersonal experiences.

Thus far, we have been imagining the case of a person trying to understand as clearly as possible the *idea* of inherent dignity, and then afterward asking if this idea is actually *true*, someone who, importantly, is open to the full range of relevant evidence, including evidence provided by the historical records of religious traditions. What has been shown is that, in embracing *inherent dignity* and *human equality* as truths, these terms are functioning at once as concepts explicable in terms of philosophical ideas, and as mythic symbols mediating faith-embraced truths about the transcendent realm of meaning and human participation in it.

Now let us step aside, so to speak, and ask about secular-minded citizens of present-day culture who do not engage in any philosophical, historical, or religious inquiry into the idea of inherent dignity, but who are nevertheless morally and politically committed to its truth. First, it seems obvious that a person doesn't need to be aware of the full range of meanings involved in the idea of inherent dignity to be moved to commitment to its truth, and to act accordingly. Second, I would argue that those for whom the concept of inherent human dignity radiates a merely secular truth in fact gain, through its embrace, an existential equilibrium that extends beyond secular social and political concerns. After all, every person lives in the cosmos, in the fullness of being, the narrative completeness of meaning, which includes the ground of reality. And although people may imagine themselves to be existing in a merely immanent universe, still an elementary awareness that reality is a cosmos—and thus that immanent being requires, in the logic of differentiating experience, a transcendent ground of being—exerts, I think, a certain pressure in every psyche.

This would help to explain why the term "dignity" has moved to the center of political discourse concerned with equality. Dignity, in the sense of inherent dignity, functions in psyches as a symbol that links the worth of all persons with the transcendent absolute that grounds their "divine equality" (Melville), not that this is recognized, of course, by the secular-minded who rely on it in this way. But so long as an *active love* of inherent human dignity helps to provide them with existential balance in the cosmos, then ignorance about the fact that dignity and equality are effectually mediating transcendent value is not dangerous.

What *is* dangerous is absence of belief in inherent dignity and human equality. "Inherent dignity" and "equality" mean nothing to those who find the ideas unconvincing, possibly because their outlooks, being reductively practicalist (as, for example, those who view humans as essentially material beings and as consumers, where those with fewer possessions have less human value), or because they hold to ideologies or worldviews wherein some people (Black, Jewish, female, Protestant, Islamic, Japanese, Roma, Slavic) are considered less human than others. And there is yet another danger, one peculiar to late modernity, in the shape of secular ideologists who emphatically embrace the idea of equal human dignity, but who imagine equality in purely material, social, and political terms, a worldly (not spiritual) equality that has yet to be constructed in history, and one that *must be made to exist*. We will return to this.

CHAPTER TWENTY

The Refusal to Understand Inherent Dignity

Inherent dignity, functioning psychologically as both concept and *mythos*, is an inspiration to many. Far fewer are those who have arrived at a clear understanding of the ideas about human nature, human participation in transcendence, and the incalculable value of personhood that are all implicit in the concept/*mythos* of inherent dignity. And fewer still are those who understand what evidence must be attended to and confirmed as sufficiently available in order to affirm, in a personal judgment, that inherent dignity is a fact, a fact that, when affirmed in personal data, is of signal importance for existential orientation. This paucity of understanding is understandable. The related set of insights involved are difficult to attain. Failures of understanding are to be expected.

But we must distinguish here between two different kinds of "failure to understand." The first kind consists of an *inability* to understand. Such inability is in no way dishonorable or shameful. The second kind of failure is another matter, because it entails a *refusal* to understand the idea of inherent dignity, and a refusal to attend to the evidence that would confirm the idea as true. Such a refusal occurs when someone who is *capable* of attaining the relevant insights turns away from that possibility by ceasing to seek both the relevant intelligibilities and the evidentiary data, and who thus *culpably* remains ignorant of the obligation to respect the inherent dignity of persons and the corresponding equality of persons. Let us consider this phenomenon.

Taken generally, culpable failures of intelligence are an important feature of human existence. Yet they receive little emphasis in contemporary culture. Why? Defining culture generally as "the set of meanings and values that informs a way of life," we can note that every culture communicates and enforces (often through the soft power of mass sentiment) disapproval of certain ideas, words, and phrases as offensive and harmful.[1] Needless to say, the winds of disapproval can change direction abruptly; certain ideas and words that yesterday were socially approved of, or accepted as anodyne, may suddenly today be prohibited.

In recent Western culture, two words that have continued to induce disapproval or unease—most dependably in the world of education—are the words "mystery," specifically as referring to a genuine metaphysical reality known to be impenetrable by human reason, and "stupidity," specifically as referring to a person's refusal to have certain insights even though he or she is capable of them. "Stupid" remains a popular term of abuse, but we are not concerned with that here. How many words are available to us, aside from "stupidity," to refer to the culpable refusal to understand, which is such an important phenomenon in personal and social life? "Stupidity" is a precise descriptor for the phenomenon, with few or no synonyms. One might be "folly."

Let us accept that there is such a thing as a culpable exercise of stupidity, and that it can occur with regard to insights of not only minor but of major significance. The refusal by stupidity to have certain moral and spiritual insights can have a decisive effect on a person's story, affecting the degree to which his or her participation in the cosmos will be able to find attunement with the ground of reality. Furthermore, this personal refusal may become politically significant. For example, a refusal of insight into inherent dignity— the value of personhood as such—can serve as a psychological bond among those who share a rejection of the *mythos* of human equality (along with related grievances and convictions), and who partly on this basis are attracted to, and adopt, a pernicious political ideology. Character-deforming stupidity—willful oversights about matters of far-reaching moral, political, and spiritual significance—has not escaped philosophical attention. Plato portrays such stupidity in a number of his dialogues. Consider the refusal of the character Alcibiades to advance to personal insights about virtue—insights he is capable of having—in Plato's *Alcibiades*, a refusal Socrates laments as "the most disgraceful form of stupidity."[2]

Among modern philosophical analyses, the clearest I am aware of is that of the Austrian novelist Robert Musil. In March 1937, Musil gave a lecture in Vienna titled "On Stupidity." The lecture begins with the assertion that there is a deep need to recover correct ideas about "freedom," "reason," and "dignity," and that success in this venture depends on understanding certain mental aberrations that undermine a healthy appreciation of these ideas. Therefore, Musil continues, "a question gradually arises that refuses to be put off: Just what *is* stupidity?"[3]

The core of his answer is as follows. There is, as we all know, Musil says, an "honorable and straightforward stupidity," which is simply a "weakness of understanding," mentioned above as the non-shameful "inability to understand."[4] But there is also a second kind, which "paradoxically, is even a sign of intelligence." This stupidity is an understanding that is "weak," so to speak, only with regard to some particular insights, "and this latter kind [of stupidity] is by far the more dangerous." Why is it so dangerous? Because this stupidity is the willful act of a person who *could*, with respect to crucial moral and spiritual matters, achieve insights, engage in sound reasoning, and apprehend genuine values, but who *avoids* insights into these particulars. This kind of stupidity, Musil indicates, is dishonorable, devious, intelligent, and dangerous. Furthermore, it can appear at the highest levels of social and political power, and can have a broad influence in the shaping of culture, even in the guidance of political or military affairs of state.

Musil calls this kind of stupidity "*intelligent* stupidity," and focuses on three of its characteristics. First, it presumes to insights and accomplishments that actually lie beyond its reach. Second, it is oriented by feelings that overrule reason in a way that creates blind spots in a person's intellectual, moral, and spiritual perspective. Third, it is endlessly inventive in using its (sometimes outstanding) intelligence to produce convincing rationalizations for its viewpoints and actions. This stupidity is the "real disease of culture," Musil says. "It reaches into the highest intellectual sphere . . . is active in every direction, and can dress up in all the clothes of truth." It is "no mental illness," yet "it is most lethal; a dangerous disease of the mind that endangers life itself."[5]

Why does it "endanger life itself?" Given the location and date of Musil's lecture—Vienna, 1937—the proximal focus of Musil's critical diagnosis is obvious. It is the rise to power and broad appeal of German National Socialism, with its aberrant vision of a revivifying and unifying culture based on a mythic sacralization of "race," "blood," and "soil," a vision with no lack of support in German and Austrian intellectual and academic circles. Of course, Musil's diagnosis applies to the intelligent stupidity that informs and supports totalitarian ideologies generally, not only in its German National Socialist but also in its Italian fascist and Bolshevik/Soviet forms.

He is alluding to deep resources of intelligence and inventiveness at the disposal of powerful leaders whose minds are diseased. Not that these leaders are "mentally ill" in a traditional psychopathological sense. And they are certainly not stupid in the simple and honorable sense. Musil is distinguishing a type of stupidity characterized by a person's distorted use of intelligence in the making of arrogant claims to knowledge regarding matters of ultimate concern, claims that involve a lethal admixture of refusals of potential insight into moral and spiritual matters and emotions unchecked by critical reason. Such stupidity obviously pertains less to intellect, Musil concludes, than to *the whole of a person's consciousness* itself. "'Intelligent' stupidity," he says, "has as its adversary not so much the understanding [as with honorable stupidity] as the *spirit* [*Geist*]."[6]

The relevance of Musil's analysis of intelligent stupidity to the national and global politics of our own time needs no elaborating. Specifically, it is useful in the diagnosis of why certain political leaders, and members of the social or political groups that support them, are dismissive or even contemptuous of the idea of basic human equality, founded as it is in the existential recognition of inherent human dignity.

CHAPTER TWENTY-ONE

Inherent Dignity and Ideology

A person's refusal to understand the idea of inherent dignity, when this is able to be understood, is principally a refusal to attend to and understand certain moral and spiritual data available in the person's own consciousness. Intelligence (sometimes the high intelligence and inventiveness of intelligent stupidity) might rationalize this refusal by forming or adopting a worldview in which the denial of human equality holds a place of honor.

The world outlook of the National Socialists led by Hitler offers a suitable example. In the race theory at the heart of this worldview, which appealed so strongly to so many in Germany (and elsewhere), different "races" carry higher or lower ontological human value. It proclaims, for example, that a person belonging to the so-called Aryan race is a more valuable being than a person belonging to, say, the "Slavic race." But a person of the "Jewish race" is of the lowest human value, or, to be more precise, in the Nazi worldview, a Jew is not of human value at all, but rather a being that is a nonworth, a sort of negative humanity, an evil counterpart to the good of human being.

The English term "worldview" translates the German *Weltanschauung*, "world outlook." The term sounds benign. But the National Socialist worldview functioned as more than just a perspective on the world that happened to have racial inequality at its core; it functioned as a systematic and total explanation about ultimate facts and values. The proper synonym for "worldview" in this case, therefore, is not "perspective on the world," but "ideology," a system of ideas through the lens of which politics, history, and human existence take on the appearance of being fully explained.

Weltanschauung (Ger.) and *idéologie* (Fr.) entered the Western cultural lexicon almost simultaneously, the former attested first in 1790, the latter in 1796. Why did the late European Enlightenment suddenly find a need for such terms? What modern developments required their creation? Most important to their invention was the emergence of the idea that humans now have within their conceptual reach—already, or through imminent advances in knowledge—a total scientific or secular comprehension of the facts that make up the meaning of existence in the world. Commonsense skepticism about the validity of such an idea was pushed aside in part by the extraordinary successes, theoretical and practical, of the natural sciences, and the consequent advance and promise of modern technologies. But the essential prelude to its being entertained as plausible was a contagious forgetfulness, especially among the so-called educated classes, about the fact that humans exist within a cosmos whose ground is a transcendent realm of meaning. Transcendent reality must be eclipsed before human beings can seriously imagine themselves capable of attaining to knowledge that explains fully what worldly existence means.

We can clarify the character of ideologies by asking, What distinguishes their aims and answers from those of properly philosophical investigation, as found in the writings of, say, Plato, Augustine, Thomas Aquinas, or Kierkegaard? The difference may be illuminated by identifying three features common to ideologies.

First, an ideology presents itself as a system that explains everything (or will eventually be able to explain everything) of basic significance to human existence. Its conceptual and methodological parts interlock, supply (or promise to supply) an answer to every important existential and historical question, and constitute a closed system, so that philosophical (and religious) exploration beyond its boundaries, including philosophical questions about human participation in a transcendent ground of meaning, is dismissed as irrelevant to significant knowledge of world and existence.

Second, ideologies accommodate no existential or ontological mysteries—such as, for example, the mystery of why a cosmos exists at all, or the mystery of why organic forms, animal life, and human existence have emerged in dynamic sequence within the cosmos, or the mystery of the goal of human history, or the mystery of the ground of being, or the mystery of evil—since recognition of such mysteries (which occurs in genuine *philosophia*) is an acknowledgment that, given free play, unrestricted human questioning leads rapidly beyond the human capacity to understand. Why does it do so? Because every existential insight gives rise to further relevant questions, and eventually the pursuit of these further questions reveals fundamental mysteries. Acknowledgment of real mysteries, however, provokes anxiety. It is a key function of every ideology to allay—at least in the short term—the anxieties that arise from revelations of mysteries.

Third, for an ideology to successfully ward off or eclipse mysteries, it must incorporate blind spots into its outlook, that is, it must ignore major data that would give the lie to its system of total explanation. Such data always include a portion of the moral and spiritual data found in the data of consciousness (i.e., in the thinker's interiority), those that, if attended to and understood, would raise questions known to be unanswerable within the closed boundary of meanings provided by the ideological system. This last point enables us to appreciate a comment Eric Voegelin made to a friend in 1957: "I just recall a splendid formula of [Austrian novelist Heimito von] Doderer's: A *Weltanschauung* is a lack of perception elevated to the rank of a system."[1]

Bringing this to bear on our concern, we can say ideologies or *Weltanschauungen* that reject the idea of inherent dignity and thus of human equality—that portray human beings, whether on political, historicist, scientific, philosophical, or religious grounds, as having *varying ontological value* depending on race, or class, or caste, or nationality, or education, or religious belief, or any other factor—evidence a failure to attain insights into those data within consciousness where the intelligibilities that give meaning to the concept of human equality are to be found. Insights into data of consciousness are set aside by scientific ideologists on principle, as irrelevant to real knowledge about the human condition, since these data are not observable through physical observation or measurable as material processes, leading "zealous practitioners of scientific method in the human field to rule out of court a major portion of the data" on human existence, Lonergan notes.[2]

But then there are those political ideologies in which equal human dignity is *not* denied, but rather embraced as a guiding principle, a principle or ideal understood to have existed in history only as a *promise*, and needing to be *created as a political fact* in the world through implementation of an ideological plan. Such ideological planning is invariably erected on two oversights. First, it fails to recognize that the equality established by inherent dignity is a spiritual truth concerning each person's participation in transcendent value, and as such is not a promise but a metaphysical fact. Second, in its presumption to complete knowledge about the essential meaning of human existence and the goals of history, it turns a blind eye to the distinction between spiritual equality and an equality imagined to be observable, and proven or disproven by way of social metrics.

Even granted the contours of its shrunken anthropological horizon, such political ideological planning faces insuperable problems. For in addition to the fact that humans regarded in terms of worldly existence do not exhibit equal talents, equal endowments, equal intelligence, and so forth, there is the capacity of mature humans to exercise their freedom for self-determination, and persons do not use their freedoms similarly and predictably. Furthermore, they often choose to *not* be just, or generous, or kind, or loving toward their fellow citizens, or compliant with authority. The unpredictable and inevitably unequal social and moral outcomes of free human self-determination (which are tolerated by political outlooks and policies that recognize and protect liberties deemed essential for personally-guided pursuits of dignified living) cannot be accommodated by ideological planners whose system requires *establishing* human equality.

Thus, wherever ideologists of equality have come to political power, as in Russia in 1917 and in Cambodia in 1975, the need to prove true the ideological rhetoric has led to the devising and implementing of policies aimed at *making* human beings "equal" by drastically curtailing their freedoms. In the Russian and Cambodian cases, this took the form of terrorizing, imprisoning, or simply killing those who didn't for various reasons fit into the ideological schema or who protested visibly against it. The attitude of the ideological believers became, "Be my brother or I will kill you." This phrase originated with Chamfort, who was describing in 1794 the French Revolutionary principle of *fraternité* as imposed during the Terror.

Political realists, as opposed to such ideologists, understand that human equality—as equal inherent dignity—cannot be other than a *spiritual* fact, which politically is reflected and enacted most essentially in the establishing of democratic self-governance and equality before the law. Government that is spiritually sensitive takes human beings as they are, protecting their inherent dignity and rights, and allowing (within legal norms) the self-shaping freedom that is the gift of participation in the transcendent ground of all freedom. Such government works to ensure equal opportunity, distributive justice, and a social safety net, but does not try to manufacture equality of achievements or destinies ("equitable outcomes") through means that end up—or even begin by—betraying inherent dignity and rights.

Ideological efforts to enforce equality are, of course, easily satirized. In a 1961 short story, Kurt Vonnegut Jr. created for them a memorable symbol: that of ballet dancers who are required to perform with heavy weights attached to them, since no one should be able to jump higher than anyone else.[3]

Epilogue
Love and Inherent Dignity

The insight that "all human beings are equal" because they share the same inherent basic dignity involves grasping that every person is, David Walsh has written, an inexhaustible center of meaning and value.[1] The invariable source of this insight is love. We have come across the definition before, but let us be clear: What is meant by "love" is not, in the first instance, a feeling but an act or state of "willing the good of the other."

Love, we recognize, involves feelings but is never reducible to feelings. Martin Buber explains the relationship between love and feelings this way: "Feelings accompany the ... fact of love, but they do not constitute it; and the feelings that accompany it can be very different. Jesus' feeling for the possessed man is different from his feeling for the beloved disciple; but the love is one."[2] How can the two loves be "one"? Not just analogously one, but *ontologically* one?

First, because in each event, Jesus wholeheartedly wills the good of the other. Who knows what feelings accompanied Jesus's love for the "beloved disciple"? Or those he felt in addressing the possessed man? But if he wills with purity of heart the particular, unique good of and for each man—the complete good that exists and is *possible* for that other—then these two "acts" of Jesus's are only *incidentally* distinct; they are *essentially* identical.

Second, because on both occasions this willing of the good *is the ground of being itself* that is manifesting itself through a person's (Jesus's) conscious love. And the ground of being is One. Someone beloved has already been found worthy of our love, but is someone like the possessed man, in whose proximity we may feel uneasy, equally worthy of our love?

If one has already accepted that equal inherent human dignity is a fact, then one needs to be able to see this man (whatever the source of his human damage) as nevertheless of incalculable inherent value, because transcendent value still shows itself through his personhood. One doesn't need to be able to act like Jesus does with the possessed man—fearlessly and with sublimely self-transcending *caritas*—in order to enter the imaginal horizon in which Jesus's response makes sense. But to enter that horizon, one does need to be able to reenact, to some degree, certain experiences that Jesus and other individuals in history must have undergone for a radical "human equality" to be envisioned, insisted upon, and promulgated (as did Paul in his Letter to the Galatians: "There is neither Jew nor Greek, slave nor free, male nor female, for you are all one in Christ Jesus."[3]

In the course of centuries, human equality eventually became the inspiration for political documents asserting the equal basic dignity and rights of all persons. History teaches us that there is nothing self-evident about human equality, in spite of famous claims to the contrary. Lonergan said that "concepts have dates." But once experiences of love for the other have occurred, the necessary insights into the meaning of those experiences have been achieved and conceptualized, and human equality has eventually been affirmed as real, no polity can justifiably ignore the inherent depth of dignity in every person, which has become its central responsibility.

Indeed, experiences of loving attunement with the universal ground of being (however symbolized, described, or incorporated into sacred traditions) are a crucial source of the emergence in history of the proclamation that every human being is of infinite value. In traditional religious language, only experiences of being loved by the one God, who wills the good of one's being absolutely and without conditions, provide an existential basis for prophets and others declaring that every person is of incalculable, irreplaceable value.

In the current world of culture and politics, *human equality* and *inherent dignity* are potent secular symbols, central to the political view that a government of, by, and for the people, based on the respect of persons as equal before the law, protecting core rights and liberties and promoting the exercise of responsible self-determination, is the best form of regime. They are the properly secular offspring—proper, since they officially recognize the inherent value of the bodily, worldly, and social dimensions of incarnate existence—of experiences of transcendent love. And though secular, unless they continue to evoke in enough members of an existing political society a concrete sense of participating in a story in which, mysteriously, every person has been given a worth beyond calculation, then the future of that order may be in danger. For in the absence of such concrete experiences, the idea of human equality remains a mere abstraction, rather than a symbol concretely mediating a living truth.

To anyone for whom the truth of "equal inherent human dignity" is merely an abstraction, allegiance to it will inevitably remain unstable. Passions may overwhelm it. Brilliant misinterpretations of human nature or human motives may subvert it. But allegiance to the equality of inherent dignity as truth is fortified when it is discovered and secured through concrete experiences of *love*: the experience of unconditionally willing the good of others and one's own good, and the experience of unrestrictedly willing the good of the ground of being itself. Then, *inherent dignity* may function as a symbol no more separable from one's sense of identity as a person than one's awareness of belonging to a cosmos.

NOTES

Chapter 1

1. Kierkegaard, *Fear and Trembling*, 200.
2. Kittredge, *Owning It All*, 177 (emphasis added).
3. Voegelin, *Israel and Revelation*, 39.
4. Kierkegaard, *The Sickness unto Death*, 13–14.

Chapter 2

1. Lonergan, *Insight*, 375.
2. Lonergan, *Insight*, see chap. 8, "Things," 270–95.
3. Voegelin, *The Ecumenic Age*, 408.
4. Mann, *Joseph the Provider*, 113.
5. Voegelin, *The Ecumenic Age*, 409–10.

Chapter 3

1. Voegelin, *Israel and Revelation*, 41.
2. Voegelin, "The Beginning and the Beyond," 221.

Chapter 4

1. Dickinson, "This world is not conclusion," 71.
2. Heidegger, *Being and Time*, 149–50, 163–68.
3. Sartre, *Existentialism Is a Humanism*, 34.

4. Heidegger, *Being and Time*, 174–75.
5. Földényi, *Dostoevsky Reads Hegel and Bursts into Tears*, 63.
6. Thomas, "A Refusal to Mourn the Death, by Fire, of a Child in London," 112.
7. Eliot, "East Coker," in *Four Quartets*, 27.
8. Gütersloh, quoted in "Sergius Pauser (1896–1970), an Austrian Painter," http://www.sergius-pauser.at/home/de.

Chapter 5

1. Buber, *I and Thou*, 102, 108–10.
2. Heidegger, *Being and Time*, 27, 67–90.
3. Aristotle, *De Anima* 429a10–430a25, in *Complete Works*, 682–84.
4. Aristotle, *De Anima* 429a15–17: "The thinking part of the soul must [have the potential to be] identical in character with its object without being the object" (*Complete Works*, 682); also *De Anima*, 430a4–5: "What thinks and what is thought are identical" (683).

Chapter 6

1. Voegelin, *Israel and Revelation*, 39.
2. Voegelin, "Anxiety and Reason," 61–67.
3. Földényi, *Dostoevsky Reads Hegel and Bursts into Tears*, 234.
4. Heer, *The Intellectual History of Europe*, 465–66.

Chapter 7

1. Lonergan, *Method in Theology*, 81–85, 265–66.
2. Voegelin, "What Is Nature?," 164.
3. *The Heart Sutra*, 2.
4. Voegelin, "The Beginning and the Beyond," 185.
5. Bly, *The Kabir Book*, 33.
6. Heraclitus's term for that which "steers" (Fragment 54) is not *nous* but *sophon* ("the wise"), suggesting a transcendent divine principle "like the Intelligence (*nous*) of Anaxagoras." See Kahn, *The Art and Thought of Heraclitus*, 55, 115.

Chapter 8

1. This chapter is largely a summary of elements of Lonergan's account of science in *Insight* and *Method in Theology*.
2. Lonergan, *Method in Theology*, 258.

3. Lonergan, *Insight*, 61–62, 65, 101–2; Lonergan, *Method in Theology*, 81–83.

Chapter 9

1. See, for example, Emmanuel Levinas, "Is Ontology Fundamental?," 8–10.
2. Wilson, *Consilience*, 297.

Chapter 10

1. Lonergan, *Insight*, chap. 12.
2. Voegelin, "What Is Political Reality?," 373–79.
3. Voegelin, "What Is Political Reality?," 396–97, 407.
4. For a summary treatment of the "basic pattern of [conscious] operations," see Lonergan, *Method in Theology*, 3–55, 104–9.
5. Lonergan, *Insight*, 34. Lonergan's phrase is "the pure question." Voegelin, *The Ecumenic Age*, 388–410, uses the capitalized "Question" to refer to the same notion.

Chapter 11

1. Sauter, "Dying with Dignity?," 291.
2. Kant, *Groundwork of the Metaphysic of Morals*, 102–3, 106–7.
3. Buber writes of "the eternal You"; see Buber, *I and Thou*.

Chapter 12

1. Cassin, quoted in Johannes Morsink, *The Universal Declaration of Human Rights: Origins, Drafting & Intent*, 287.
2. Mary Ann Glendon, *A World Made New*, 146 (emphasis added).

Chapter 14

1. Lonergan, *Insight*, 271, 461.

Chapter 15

1. See Victor E. Frankl, *Man's Search for Meaning*.
2. Voegelin, "The Gospel and Culture," in Voegelin, *Published Essays, 1966–1985*, 176.

3. Lonergan, *Insight*, 210–12.
4. Hegel, *Aesthetics: Lectures on Fine Art*, 1228.
5. Lonergan, *Insight*, 237.
6. For example, *Nicomachean Ethics* 1113a30–31, 4.3.
7. Nietzsche, *Beyond Good and Evil*, 81 (Aphorism 78).

Chapter 16

1. Dickinson, "A nearness to tremendousness," 362.
2. Kahn, *The Art and Thought of Heraclitus*, 45 (Fr. 35).
3. Philo, quoted in E. M. Forster, *Alexandria*, 58.
4. Fedoryka, "The Ontological and Existential Dimensions of Human Dignity," 122.
5. Levinas, *Humanism of the Other*, 44.
6. Kant, *Groundwork*, 103, 106, 107.
7. Joas, *The Sacredness of the Person*, see esp. 49–64, 140–70.

Chapter 17

1. Patočka, *Heretical Essays*, 41.
2. Patočka, *Heretical Essays*, 41, 77.
3. Patočka, *Heretical Essays*, 50, 102, 104.
4. Patočka, *Heretical Essays*, 25–26, 43, 102, 108.
5. Havel, "Human Rights," speech delivered on June 29, 1995, at the inauguration of the Human Rights Building in Strasbourg; https://muzeuminternetu.cz/offwebs/czech/364.htm.
6. Voegelin, "What Is Political Reality?," 396.
7. Patočka, *Heretical Essays*, 43, 131, 134–35.

Chapter 18

1. Kabir, *The Weaver's Songs*, 162.
2. Yakovlev, *The Fate of Marxism in Russia*, 202.
3. Hill, quoted in Lee Oser, *Christian Humanism in Shakespeare*, 51.
4. Trotsky, quoted in Martin Amis, *Koba the Dread*, 35.
5. Rosenstock-Huessy, *Out of Revolution*, 51.
6. Lenin, quoted in Paul Froese, *The Plot to Kill God*, 44.
7. Yakovlev, *A Century of Violence in Soviet Russia*, xv.

Chapter 19

1. Melville, *Moby Dick*, 123 (chap. 26).

2. Voegelin, *Hitler and the Germans*, 205.
3. Voegelin, *Hitler and the Germans*, 204.
4. Kant, *Groundwork*, 102.

Chapter 20

1. Lonergan, *Method in Theology*, xi.
2. Plato, *Alcibiades* 117a–118b (p. 575).
3. Musil, "On Stupidity," 268.
4. Musil, "On Stupidity," 282.
5. Musil, "On Stupidity," 283–84.
6. Musil, "On Stupidity," 285.

Chapter 21

1. Voegelin, Letter to Robert Heilman, February 23, 1957; in Voegelin, *Selected Correspondence, 1950–1984*, 306.
2. Lonergan, *Insight*, 260.
3. Vonnegut, "Harrison Bergeron," 857–62.

Epilogue

1. See, for example, Walsh, "Dignity as an Eschatological Concept," 123–36.
2. Buber, *I and Thou*, 33.
3. Galatians 3:28.

BIBLIOGRAPHY

Amis, Martin. *Koba the Dread: Laughter and the Twenty Million.* New York: Talk Miramax Books, 2002.
Aristotle. *De Anima.* In *The Complete Works of Aristotle,* Vol.1, edited by Jonathan Barnes and translated by J. A. Smith, 641–92. Princeton, NJ: Princeton University Press, 1984.
———. *Nicomachean Ethics.* In *The Complete Works of Aristotle,* Vol. 2, edited by Jonathan Barnes and translated by J. A. Smith, 1729–1867. Princeton, NJ: Princeton University Press, 1984.
Bly, Robert, trans. *The Kabir Book: Forty-Four of the Ecstatic Poems of Kabir.* Boston: Beacon Press, 1977.
Buber, Martin. *I and Thou.* Translated by Walter Kaufmann. New York: Charles Scribner's Sons, 1970.
Dickinson, Emily. "A nearness to tremendousness." In *The Poems of Emily Dickinson,* 362.
———. "This world is not conclusion." In *The Poems of Emily Dickinson: Reading Edition,* edited by R. W. Franklin, 71. Cambridge, MA: Belknap Press of Harvard University Press, 1999.
Eliot, T. S. "East Coker." In *Four Quartets.* London: Faber & Faber, 1944.
Fedoryka, Damian P. "The Ontological and Existential Dimensions of Human Dignity." In *Menschenwürde: Metaphysik und Ethik,* edited by Mariano Crespo, 119–44. Heidelberg: Carl Winter University, 1998.
Földényi, László. *Dostoevsky Reads Hegel and Bursts into Tears.* Translated by Ottilie Mulzet. New Haven, CT: Yale University Press, 2020.
Forster, E. M. *Alexandria: A History and Guide, and Pharos and Pharillon.* Edited by Miriam Allott. London: Andre Deutsch, 2004.
Frankl, Victor E. *Man's Search for Meaning.* Boston: Beacon Press, 2006.
Froese, Paul. *The Plot to Kill God: Findings from the Soviet Experiment in Secularization.* Berkeley: University of California Press, 2008.

Glendon, Mary Ann. *A World Made New: Eleanor Roosevelt and the Universal Declaration of Human Rights.* New York: Random House, 2001.

Havel, Václav. "Human Rights." Speech delivered at the inauguration of the Human Rights Building, Strasbourg, France, June 29, 1995. https://muzeum internetu.cz/offwebs/czech/364.htm.

Heer, Friedrich, *The Intellectual History of Europe.* Translated by Jonathan Steinberg. Cleveland: The World Publishing Company, 1953.

Hegel, Georg Wilhelm Friedrich. *Aesthetics: Lectures on Fine Art*, Vol. 2. Translated by Thomas M. Knox. Oxford: Oxford University Press, 1975.

Heidegger, Martin. *Being and Time.* Translated by John Macquarrie and Edward Robinson. New York: Harper & Row, 1962.

Hill, Geoffrey. *Collected Critical Writings.* Edited by Kenneth Haynes. Oxford: Oxford University Press, 2009.

Joas, Hans. *The Sacredness of the Person: A New Genealogy of Human Rights.* Translated by A. Skinner. Washington, DC: Georgetown University Press, 2013.

Kabir. *The Weaver's Songs.* Translated by Vinay Dharwadker. London: Penguin Books, 2003.

Kahn, Charles H., trans. and commentary. *The Art and Thought of Heraclitus: An Edition of the Fragments with Translation and Commentary.* Cambridge: Cambridge University Press, 1981.

Kant, Immanuel. *Groundwork of the Metaphysic of Morals.* Translated by H. J. Paton. New York: Harper & Row, 1964.

Kierkegaard, Søren. *Fear and Trembling/Repetition.* Edited and translated by Howard V. Hong and Edna H. Hong. Princeton, NJ: Princeton University Press, 1983.

——. *The Sickness unto Death: A Christian Psychological Exposition for Upbuilding and Awakening.* Edited and translated by Howard V. Hong and Edna H. Hong. Princeton, NJ: Princeton University Press, 1980.

Kittredge, William. *Owning It All: Essays.* Minneapolis: Graywolf Press, 1987.

Levinas, Emmanuel. "Is Ontology Fundamental?" In *Basic Philosophical Writings*, edited by Adriaan T. Peperzak, Simon Critchley, and Robert Bernascone, 1–10. Bloomington: Indiana University Press, 1996.

——. *Humanism of the Other.* Translated by Nidra Poller. Urbana: University of Illinois Press, 2006.

Lonergan, Bernard. *Insight: A Study of Human Understanding.* Edited by Frederick E. Crowe and Robert M. Doran. Toronto: University of Toronto Press, 1992.

——. *Method in Theology.* New York: Herder and Herder, 1972.

Mann, Thomas. *Joseph the Provider.* Trans. H. T. Lowe-Porter. New York: Alfred A. Knopf, 1944.

Melville, Herman. *Moby Dick; or, The Whale.* New York: The Heritage Press, 1943.

Morsink, Johannes. *The Universal Declaration of Human Rights: Origins, Drafting & Intent.* Philadelphia: University of Pennsylvania Press, 1999.

Musil, Robert. "On Stupidity." In *Precision and Soul: Essays and Addresses*, translated and edited by Burton Pike and David S. Luft, 268–86. Chicago: University of Chicago Press, 1990.
Nietzsche, Friedrich. *Beyond Good and Evil: Prelude to a Philosophy of the Future*. Translated by Walter Kaufmann. New York: Vintage Books, 1989.
Oser, Lee. *Christian Humanism in Shakespeare: A Study in Religion and Literature*. Washington, DC: Catholic University of America Press, 2022.
Patočka, Jan. *Heretical Essays in the Philosophy of History*. Translated by Erazim Kohák and edited by James Dodd. Chicago: Open Court, 1996.
Plato. *Alcibiades*. In *Plato: Complete Works*, edited by John M. Cooper and translated by D. S. Hutchinson. Indianapolis: Hackett, 1997.
———. *Phaedo*. In *Plato: Complete Works*.
Red Pine, trans. and commentary. *The Heart Sutra*. Washington, DC: Shoemaker & Hoard, 2004.
Rosenstock-Huessy, Eugen. *Out of Revolution: Autobiography of Western Man*. Providence, RI: Berg Publishers, 1993.
Sartre, Jean-Paul. *Existentialism Is a Humanism*. Translated by Philip Mairet. London: Methuen Books, 1948.
Sauter, Gerhard. "Dying with Dignity?" In *God and Human Dignity*, edited by R. Kendall Soulen and Linda Woodhead, 282–96. Grand Rapids, MI: William B. Eerdmans, 2006.
Thomas, Dylan. "A Refusal to Mourn the Death, by Fire, of a Child in London." In *Collected Poems*. New York: New Directions, 1957.
Voegelin, Eric. "Anxiety and Reason." In *The Collected Works of Eric Voegelin*, Vol. 28, *"What Is History?" and Other Late Unpublished Writings*, edited by Thomas A. Hollweck and Paul Caringella, 52–110. Baton Rouge: Louisiana State University Press, 1990.
———. "The Beginning and the Beyond: A Meditation on Truth." In *The Collected Works of Eric Voegelin*, 28:173–232.
———. *The Ecumenic Age: Order and History* (Vol. 4). Vol. 17 of *The Collected Works of Eric Voegelin*. Edited by Michael Franz. Columbia: University of Missouri Press, 2000.
———. "The Gospel and Culture." In *The Collected Works of Eric Voegelin*, Vol. 12, *Published Essays, 1966–1985*, edited by Ellis Sandoz, 172–212. Baton Rouge: Louisiana State University Press, 1990.
———. *Hitler and the Germans*, Vol. 31 of *The Collected Works of Eric Voegelin*. Translated by Detlev Clemens and edited by Brendan Purcell. Columbia: University of Missouri Press, 1999.
———. *Israel and Revelation: Order and History* (Vol. 1). Vol. 14 of *The Collected Works of Eric Voegelin*. Edited by Maurice P. Hogan. Columbia: University of Missouri Press, 2001.
———. Letter to Robert Heilman, February 23, 1957. In *The Collected Works of Eric Voegelin*, Vol. 30, *Selected Correspondence, 1950–1984*, translated by Sandy Adler, Thomas A. Hollweck, and William Petropulos and edited by Thomas A. Hollweck, 304–7. Columbia: University of Missouri Press, 2007.

———. "What Is Nature?" In *The Collected Works of Eric Voegelin*, Vol. 6, *Anamnesis: On the Theory of History and Politics*, edited by David Walsh and translated by M. J. Hanak, 157–74. Columbia: University of Missouri Press, 2002.

———. "What Is Political Reality?" In *The Collected Works of Eric Voegelin*, 6:341–412. Columbia, MO: University of Missouri Press, 2002

Vonnegut, Kurt. "Harrison Bergeron." In *Complete Stories*, 857–62. New York: Seven Stories Press, 2017.

Wilson, E. O. *Consilience*. London: Abacus, 1998.

Yakovlev, Alexander N. *A Century of Violence in Soviet Russia*. Translated by Anthony Austin. New Haven, CT: Yale University Press, 2002.

———. *The Fate of Marxism in Russia*. Translated by Catherine A. Fitzpatrick. New Haven, CT: Yale University Press, 1993.

INDEX

A
achieved dignity, 74–78
Anaxagoras, 116n6 (chap. 7)
Aristotle, 38, 42
   on cognition, 22–23, 116n4 (chap. 5)
   on happiness, 69
   and *spoudaios*, 78
   See also form
Artaud, Antonin, 29
artificial intelligence, 44
attunement, 17, 24, 42, 92, 103, 112.
      See also cosmos

B
Bolshevik. *See* ideology
boundlessness. *See also* Dickinson,
    Emily
Brahman, 17, 30, 31, 45, 99
   as impersonal, 58–59
Breivik, Anders. *See* ideology
Buber, Martin, 21
   on love, 111
   Thou, 59, 89, 117n3 (chap. 11)
Buddhism, 28, 45, 59
   Heart Sutra, 32

C
Cassin, René, 62, 63, 66, 67
cause
   formal, 5
   material, 5
   not of own self, 5, 15, 49
   ontological, 6
certitude, 82, 87–88
   activists of, 92, 95
   as eclipse of transcendence, 91–92
Chamfort, Sébastien-Roch, 110
Chang, P. C., 63, 66, 67
communion. *See* identity
consciousness, 18, 37, 77
   acts of, 39, 41
   compact, 11–12
   data of, 35, 39, 49, 98, 100. 106, 108
   and desire to know, 7, 22, 40, 48
   differentiation of, 11, 12, 45, 58
   as embodied, 4
   and emergence, 9, 58
   as integration, 72
   self-, 76
   as spirit, 40
   and stupidity, 105
   as tension, 48–49
   and transcendence, 41, 45, 47, 58,
      72, 79, 92
   See also Voegelin, Eric
consubstantiality. *See* cosmos

cosmos
  attunement to, 26, 75
  compactness of, 12
  and consubstantiality, 12
  differentiation of, 11, 12, 30, 45, 58, 59
  as foundational experience, 32, 36, 100, 108
  as lost, 13–14, 88, 107
  micro-, 41
  order of, 27
  partial understanding of, 91
  and participation, 17, 26, 29, 39, 45, 48, 75, 84, 87, 103
  as replaced, 13
  tale of, 26, 28
  and transcendence, 42
  ultimate basis of, 49
  as Whole, 11, 12, 13, 16, 30, 31, 32, 34, 45, 48, 71, 72
  See also ground; myth
courtesy. *See* ground

D
de Sade, Marquis Donatien Alphonse, 79
Dickinson, Emily, 15, 29
  and boundlessness, 82
differentiation
  of experiences, 57, 100
  of meaning, 13, 27, 30, 48
  and religion, 28–29, 34, 48
  See also cosmos
dignitas, 66
disruption. *See* Patočka, Jan
divine reality
  and equality, 96, 101
  as ground, 47
  as intelligence, 34, 42, 82, 116n6 (chap. 7)
  as mystery, 13, 69
  participation in, 11–12, 42, 58
  as personhood, 59, 75
  presence of, 31, 36, 37, 59, 67, 98
  and society, 31
  and transcendence, 12, 30, 33, 34, 67
  See also freedom; identity; love

Dostoevsky, Fyodor, 79
Drama of humanity, 9, 36

E
Eliot, T. S., 18, 42
equality
  absence of belief in, 101
  absent in Hinduism, 99
  and ideology, 93, 101, 105, 108, 109
  and liberal democracy, 98, 113
  as mythic symbol, 100
  not self-evident, 112
  ontological, 81, 84
  refusal to understand, 103, 105, 106
  spiritual, 97, 109–10
  and transcendence, 81, 93, 95
  See also nature; rights; Universal Declaration of Human Rights
eschatology
  and transcendence, 12, 28
  and yearning, 10, 14

F
Fedoryka, Damian, 83
Földényi, László, 18
forgetfulness, 32, 82, 107
form
  as cause, 5
  in *Heart Sutra*, 33
  and intelligibility, 23
  natural, 32
  in Plato, Aristotle, and Aquinas, 23
Frankl, Viktor, 76
freedom
  denial of transcendent source of, 79
  divine, 18, 21, 23, 66, 67
  as essence of human, 9, 44, 56, 77, 78, 97, 98
  ground of, 110
  and ideology, 93, 109
  and liberal democracy, 67
  and responsibility, 73
  and participation, 110
  and self-determination, 17, 20, 73, 74, 109, 110
  as spiritual, 45, 79, 88
  and understanding, 21

Index 127

G
ground
  of being, 25, 27, 29, 47, 49, 72, 84, 88–90, 99, 113
  of cosmos, 13, 16, 18, 20, 40, 87
  courtesy toward, 18–19
  knowledge of the, 92
  identity with, 6
  is One, 112
  of own existence, 17, 18
  mystery of, 13, 15, 17, 19, 29, 45, 48, 91, 108
  transcendent, 13, 23, 27, 31, 32, 42, 57, 79, 82, 88, 100–101, 107
  See also freedom
Gütersloh, A. P., 19

H
Havel, Václav, 88
Heart Sutra. See Buddhism; form; paradox
Heer, Friedrich, 29
Heidegger, Martin, 16, 17, 21
Heraclitus, 17, 34, 116n6 (chap. 7)
heuristic, 8, 9, 16, 74, 78
  intrinsically, 68–70
Hill, Geoffrey, 94
Hinduism, 28, 33, 92. *See also* Brahman

I
identity
  and communion, 19, 25, 28
  divine, 30
  personal, 73, 113
  with transcendence, 58
  unity-, 8, 72, 82
  See also ground
ideology, 18, 101, 104, 109, 110
  Bolshevik, 44, 92–95
  and Breivik, Anders, 84–85
  distinguished from philosophy, 107–8
  synonyms for, 107
immanence
  and intelligible structures, 36–37
  as realm of meaning, 19
  and transcendence, 13, 31, 32–34, 40, 43, 45, 48, 58, 59, 100
immanentism, 18, 43–45
in-between, 48
intelligence
  artificial, 44
  failures of, 103–5, 106
  and the intelligible, 22, 40, 49–50
  as participation in reality, 5
  See also divine reality

J
Jesus, 111, 112
Joas, Hans, 85

K
Kabir, 33–34, 92
Kant, Immanuel, 43, 84, 99
  on dignity, 58, 67
Kierkegaard, Søren, 3, 5, 77, 86, 107

L
La Mettrie, Julien Offray de, 43–44
Lenin, Vladimir Ilyich, 92, 94
Levinas, Emmanuel, 42, 83
liberal democracy, 67, 81, 84, 94. *See also* equality; freedom
Logos, 17, 30, 82
Lonergan, Bernard, 8, 112
  constancy of cognitional structure, 49–51
  living as drama, 77
  and science, 37
  and scientism, 108–9
  unity-identity-whole, 72
love
  active, 101
  acts of loving, 8, 24, 48, 51, 73, 88
  and belonging, 18
  definition of, 83
  divine, 75, 112
  as heuristic, 69
  as human potentiality, 83, 97, 98–99
  as more than feeling, 111–12
  of oneself, 84
  as participation, 66

love (*cont.*)
   refusal of, 109
   and transcendence, 13, 113
   See also Buber, Martin; values

M
Malik, Charles, 63, 66, 67
Mann, Thomas, 9
meaning
   and intelligibility, 7–10, 22–23, 31
   and mystery, 9
   narrative completeness of, 11, 12, 14, 16, 18, 36, 91, 100
   and the person, 111
   and reality, 5, 11
   realms of, 11–12, 13, 30–31, 32, 41, 48
   scientific, 37–39
   search for, 48–49
   and transcendence, 18, 31, 33, 40, 57–58, 72, 87–88, 92, 100, 107
   See also immanence
Melville, Herman, 96, 98, 101
Micah, 17
Mitchell, Joni, 15
modernity, 18, 28, 97, 98, 101
Musil, Robert, 104–5
mystery, 9
   and anxiety, 108
   belonging to, 17, 18
   of history, 91
   and human value, 68, 84
   of Incarnation, 90
   and participation, 69
   and the person, 88, 90, 113
   and resistance to, 92–93, 95, 103, 108
   transcendent, 12, 14, 28, 79, 81–82, 89, 90
   See also divine reality; ground; meaning; reason; Voegelin, Eric
myth
   aberrant, 105
   and cosmos, 26–28, 45
   early, 12–13
   and the moderns, 28–29
   and Plato, 69
   secular, 29
   and transcendence, 28, 98, 100
   See also equality; politics; symbol

N
National Socialism, 61, 105, 106
nature
   and constants, 48
   and differentiation, 30–31
   and equality, 58
   realm of, 39
   relative autonomy of, 35
   and transcendent reality, 32
   See also Universal Declaration of Human Rights
Nietzsche, Friedrich, 78
nous
   as human participation in divine, 34, 42, 58
   as transcendent reality, 45, 116n6 (chap. 7)

P
paradox, 12, 19
   and *Heart Sutra*, 32
Parmenides, 34
participation, 5
   and human existence, 43, 47, 77, 87
   and personhood, 19, 40, 75, 88, 109
   perspective of, 8, 9
   in process of reality, 48, 72
   in transcendence, 23, 28, 47, 57, 58, 79, 93, 98, 99–100, 102
   See cosmos; divine reality; freedom; intelligence; love; *nous*; mystery; Voegelin, Eric
Patočka, Jan, 87–88
   on disruption, 88, 90
personhood
   acts of, 23, 73
   and nonhuman reality, 71
   and process of reality, 24
   and reverence, 84–85
   and transcendent reality, 72

and Trinity, 59
value of, 73–75, 102, 103, 112
See also divine reality; identity; meaning; mystery; participation; rights
Philo, 82
Plato, 17, 34, 42, 107
  Phaedo, 39–40
  on stupidity, 104
  See also form; myth
politics
  and culture, xvii
  and dignity, 57, 58, 60, 86, 98, 100–101, 113
  and friendship, 18
  and ideology, 104–5, 109–10
  independence of, 31
  influence of UNDR, 64–65, 67, 68
  and myth, 29
  and theory, xvii
process of reality. *See* participation; personhood

Q
questioner, 3, 10, 97
questioning
  aiming at insight, 49
  and desire to know, 7–8, 9
  fruition of, 51
  radical, 88
  science as mode of, 36
  as unrestricted, 15–16, 91, 108

R
reason
  as act of consciousness, 98
  mystery as impenetrable to, 103
  nobility of, 66–67
  and stupidity, 104–5
  trustworthiness of, 16
  universality of, 68
  See also nous
remembrance, 18, 19, 45
rights
  Commission on Human Rights, 61, 67
  connection with dignity, 55, 57, 59, 62–63, 73–74
  and duties, 74
  and equality, 58, 112
  and government, 110, 113
  inherent, 57
  and personhood, 73
  and U.S. Declaration of Independence, 62
  World Conference on Human Rights, 64
  See also Universal Declaration of Human Rights
Roosevelt, Eleanor, 63, 66
Rosenstock-Huessy, Eugen, 94

S
Sartre, Jean-Paul, 17
Sauter, Gerhard, 57
secularism
  and symbols, 113
  without transcendent meaning, 36, 99
  truth and, 100–101, 107
  See also myth; Universal Declaration of Human Rights
spirit
  body and, 39
  divine, 58
  as self, 23–24
  See also consciousness
stupidity. *See* Musil, Robert; Plato; reason
symbol
  and dignity, 100
  as heuristic, 68
  language, 65
  and myth, 26, 29, 100
  need for, 28
  and the person, 66, 68
  and religious experience, 33
  See also equality; secularism

T
Tao, 17, 30, 31, 32, 45, 59
Te Water, C. T., 63

transcendence. *See* certitude; consciousness; cosmos; divine reality; equality; eschatology; freedom; ground; identity; immanence; love; meaning; mystery; myth; nature; *nous*; participation; personhood; secularism; Voegelin, Eric
Trotsky, Leon, 94

U
United Nations, 61
Universal Declaration of Human Rights (UDHR)
    composition of committee, 63
    and dignity, 67–68, 70, 73–74
    and equality, 67
    influence of, 64
    and inherent dignity, 63
    and nature, 62, 68
    ratification of, 61
    secular character of, 62
    See also politics
universal humanity, 9

V
values
    and culture, 103
    as moral meanings, 7
    and love, 51
    "unalterable," 64
Voegelin, Eric, 26, 27, 49, 97
    and consciousness, 12, 48
    and drama of living, 5, 9
    on mystery, 89
    on participation, 77
    on primary experience, 32
    on transcendence, 33
    on *Weltanschaaung*, 108
Vonnegut, Kurt, Jr., 110

W
Walsh, David, 111, 119n1 (epilogue)
Weltanschaaung, 107–8
Wilson, E. O., 44

Y
Yahweh, 30
Yakovlev, Alexander, 93

Glenn Hughes (1951–2024) was professor emeritus at St. Mary's University. He was the inaugural holder of the St. Mary's Chair in Catholic Philosophy. He is the author of several books including *From Dickinson to Dylan* and *Transcendence and History*.

www.ingramcontent.com/pod-product-compliance
Lightning Source LLC
Chambersburg PA
CBHW031834230426
43669CB00009B/1353